MEMBER ASSISTANCE PROGRAMS IN THE WORKPLACE

THE ROLE OF LABOR IN THE PREVENTION AND TREATMENT OF SUBSTANCE ABUSE

Samuel B. Bacharach
Peter Bamberger
William J. Sonnenstuhl

ILR Bulletin 69

ILR Press
an imprint of
Cornell University Press
Ithaca and London

First published 1994 by ILR Press.
Second printing 1995 by ILR Press/Cornell University Press.

Bacharach, Samuel B.
    Member assistance programs in the workplace : the role of labor in
  the prevention and treatment of substance abuse / Samuel B.
  Bacharach, Peter Bamberger, William J. Sonnenstuhl.
       p.   cm.—(ILR bulletin ; 69)
  Includes bibliographical references.
  ISBN 0-87546-336-3
    1. Employee assistance programs. 2. Employees—Counseling of.
  3. Peer counseling. 4. Trade-unions. 5. Alchoholism and employment.
  6. Drugs and employment.   I. Bamberger, Peter. II. Sonnenstuhl,
  William J., 1946– . III. Title. IV. Series: Bulletin (New York
  State School of Industrial and Labor Relations) ; no. 69.
  HF5549.5.E42B33 1994
658.3'82   94-31790

Printed in the United States of America

♾ The paper in this book meets the minimum requirements of the
American National Standard for Information Sciences—Permanence of
Paper for Printed Library Materials, ANSI Z39.48-1984.

CONTENTS

Preface / *v*

Introduction / *1*

1   Origins and Goals of Member Assistance Programs / *7*

2   MAPs in the Transportation Industry / *14*

3   Establishing and Maintaining an MAP / *27*

4   Providing Help and Referral / *48*

5   Follow-up and Reintegration into the Workplace / *60*

6   Prevention through Cultural Change / *74*

7   Summary and Policy Implications / *79*

References / *83*

PREFACE

Although this bulletin tells the story of labor's role in the prevention and treatment of substance abuse, it is also about what individuals, acting together, can do. Member Assistance Programs (MAPs), which are labor-based peer counseling and referral programs, are built upon a spirit of communal voluntarism, a belief that people can solve their problems by working together. While communal voluntarism is the basis of effective MAPs, it is also a deeply embedded belief in American culture. It is the basis of American government, something most evident in New England town meetings, and it is the basis of Americans' attraction to self-help groups as a mechanism for solving both individual and social problems. Consequently, our story about what union members are doing to help those who suffer from substance abuse and other personal problems should be read with an eye to its wider implications for solving America's social problems.

In this bulletin we use the terms *member assistance* and *peer counseling* conceptually, that is, we use the term *member assistance* to denote any labor-based activity in which co-workers act to either prevent substance abuse problems or refer chemically dependent or other troubled co-workers to community resources for help (i.e., self-help groups or professional treatment programs). Thus, according to our use of the term, both the CSXT and Amtrak Operation:RedBlock Programs, in which union members focus primarily upon the prevention of substance abuse problems, and the Association of Flight Attendants Employee Assistance Program, in which union members focus on the identification and referral of troubled co-workers, are defined as member assistance programs. Similarly, we use the term *peer counselor* to denote the union volunteers who perform the prevention role in Operation:RedBlock and the referral role in the Association of Flight

Attendants Employee Assistance Program. Both programs are put forth as excellent examples of what peers can accomplish in the area of substance abuse prevention and treatment. We argue, however, that ultimately, effective MAPs must integrate the best features of both in order to create comprehensive substance abuse programs capable of deterring alcohol and other drug use, ensuring appropriate treatment for chemically dependent workers, and ensuring members' long-term abstinence and sobriety.

Our study finds that well-implemented MAPs have a major role to play in the prevention and treatment of substance abuse problems. In particular, they promise to be a crucial mechanism for the transformation of those occupational cultures that have historically been supportive of substance abuse. These cultures, as we explain, developed as one way some occupational groups have sought to construct a sense of solidarity in opposition to management efforts to control their work. Because of this history, such occupational cultures have been highly resistant to management change. As the case of Operation:RedBlock illustrates, however, peer efforts to change their own culture can have a dramatic impact.

In addition, peers also have important roles to play in helping their co-workers receive substance abuse treatment and maintain long-term abstinence and sobriety. Indeed, as the case of the Association of Flight Attendants Employee Assistance Program illustrates, well-trained peer counselors are instrumental to an effective program. They provide co-workers suffering from substance abuse as well as other personal problems valuable and timely information about their problems and the community resources available for solving their problems. At the same time, they provide co-workers the crucial ingredient for ensuring long-term abstinence and sobriety: ongoing social support both on and off the job.

Although we are enthusiastic about the contributions that MAPs make to the prevention and treatment of substance abuse, we do not want to imply criticism of well-run management-sponsored employee assistance programs (EAPs). Rather, as we state in the bulletin, well-implemented MAPs often must interact with EAPs, and it is to the advantage of both programs, as well as the workers they seek to help, to work out a cooperative relationship with one another. When highly adversarial labor-management relations make this infeasible, unions may have to act unilaterally to provide their members an effective program.

EAPs in nonunion settings may also wish to develop their own peer counseling networks to enhance their programs. Like MAPs, early EAPs also drew on an ethic of communal voluntarism, as recovering alcoholics began helping their co-workers suffering from alcoholism. But as the programs have become increasingly accepted within the American workplace, they have also become more bureaucratized and professionalized, characteristics that work against the spirit of communal voluntarism. One way to reinvigorate EAPs with the ethic of communal voluntarism is to introduce peer counselors into these programs. Indeed, many of the functions that peers fulfill within an MAP can also be served within EAPs, and we hope that our readers will begin exploring such possibilities.

This bulletin was made possible by the efforts of a number of organizations and people. We are particularly indebted to the three organizations that allowed us access to their peer counselors and members, the Association of Flight Attendants, Amtrak, and CSX Transportation, and we wish to extend our thanks to them. A number of individuals from these organizations were particularly helpful in helping us to understand how their programs work. In particular, we should like to thank Bobby Bonds, Daniel Collins, Sr., Jerry Davis, Dr. Barbara Feuer, Sherrie Mirsky, Eric Pack, Malva Reid, Palma Seeger, Dennis Sullivan, Richard Taylor, and William Wick. In addition, we owe a special thanks to Valerie Kennedy, who conducted fieldwork on Operation:RedBlock; Colleen Clauson, who helped us coordinate the numerous tasks of coordinating a major research project such as this; and Erica Fox, who edited the manuscript. We also thank Frances Benson, director of ILR Press, Holly Bailey, and Faith Short for their input. In addition, Bryan Mundell played a central role in helping us crystallize our ideas and get them down on paper. Our greatest debt, however, is to the men and women of these organizations who generously shared their stories with us so that others might learn how peer-based programs can prevent and treat substance abuse.

Finally, we would like to acknowledge our debt to and appreciation of the National Institute on Drug Abuse, which supported our research efforts (DA 06995-03).* Without its support, this project would not have come to fruition. We specifically want to thank Helen Cesare, who served as project officer. We hope that this work will reinforce the conviction that the social sciences have a concrete and important role in the development of substance abuse prevention and treatment policies.

---

*All authors contributed equally to both the study and the preparation of this book, and thus the names appear in alphabetical order.

INTRODUCTION

Americans are ambivalent about the meaning of community in their lives (Hewitt 1989). Communities represent order, and we long for their comforting embrace. They are protective places to which we turn for emotional support. But many Americans also see communities as stifling, as something from which they wish to escape. From this perspective, communities force their standards on us, snuffing out our individuality. Although some social critics fear that Americans have permanently escaped from a sense of community into a preoccupation with self (e.g., Lasch 1978), others argue that we continue to long for a feeling of community and struggle to reconstruct it in our daily lives (Gusfield 1975; Cohen 1985; Bellah et al. 1991; Etzioni 1991).

In the United States, communalism and individualism represent deep-rooted and persistent polarities in modes of thought, feeling, and action (Erikson 1976). According to social historians, to create a balance between communalism and individualism, Americans experience cycles in which the virtues of society and of self are alternately extolled and rejected. This polarity is most evident when we are experiencing problems, and it may be observed in the way we talk about them.

Historically, drinking represents Americans' ambivalence toward communalism and individualism (Lender and Martin 1987). On the one hand, Americans see drinking rituals, such as toasting a bride and groom and taking communion, as solidifying communal bonds. On the other hand, they view drinking as selfish and as sowing the seeds of major social disruptions, such as murder and economic downturns. Some conceive of it as a necessary time-out from the hectic bustle of the modern world (Gusfield 1987). Others see it as destroying our fragile sense of community (Gusfield 1981). Still others are ambivalent; they view drinking as socially acceptable but potentially dangerous and therefore requiring care and awareness (Beauchamp 1980).

Some Americans have historically blamed intemperate or irresponsible drinking for creating our social problems. According to this view, intemperate drinking disrupts our social life, and irresponsible drinkers, whether defined as drunkards or alcoholics, are folk devils (Cohen 1972) whose selfish pursuit of alcohol must be controlled if a sense of community is to be maintained and our social problems resolved (Ben-Yehuda 1990).

Since the beginning of the nineteenth century, America has undergone five cycles of temperance reform (Blocker 1989). During each period, some groups, such as the Women's Christian Temperance Union and Mothers against Drunk Drivers, have attributed America's social problems, from poverty to death at the hands of drunk drivers, to the intemperate use of alcohol and have sought to reform problem drinkers (Gusfield 1963, 1981). These groups initially sought to persuade problem drinkers to change their behavior by teaching them to drink responsibly or abstain. When persuasion failed, the reformers pursued coercive techniques to force the drinkers to be socially responsible, including enacting legislation prohibiting the sale of alcoholic beverages.

Typically, each cycle of reform ended when Americans began to experience the coercive techniques as restraining their sense of individuality, and they advocated loosening the social controls. National prohibition was brought to an abrupt end, for instance, when businesspeople who had originally lobbied for its passage organized and pressed for the repeal of prohibition because they feared a government so strong that it could wipe out an entire industry (Kyvig 1979).

Today, America is in the midst of another cycle of temperance reform. It differs from earlier cycles in that Americans no longer view alcohol as the only cause of the destruction of society but focus on legal and illegal substances generally (Ames 1989). This shift occurred in the 1960s when American middle-class youth began to experiment with illicit drugs, especially marijuana (Beauchamp 1980; Lidz and Walker 1980; Goode 1989). Nonetheless, the struggle parallels earlier reform efforts (Levine and Reinarman 1993) in that some Americans perceive drug and alcohol use as the means by which to create a sense of community, while others decry the use of drugs and alcohol for turning generations into zombies and undermining the public good.

Simultaneously, public debate has focused on how to reform those who use and abuse drugs and alcohol. Proposals for reform vary from the persuasive (campaigns to teach children to "Just Say No!" and programs that provide voluntary treatment to substance abusers) to the coercive (drug testing, imprisonment of drug users, and compulsory treatment for drug dependence) (Bayer and Oppenheimer 1993; Shoemaker 1989).

Until the 1970s, most substance abuse programs in the United States were informal, community-based, voluntary self-help groups, such as Alcoholics Anonymous (AA). Today, such programs are part of a complex medical bureaucracy and are staffed by an increasing array of professionals, including psychologists, social workers, certified alcoholism counselors, and credentialed employee assistance workers (Lender and Martin 1987; Blocker 1989).

But even as substance abuse treatment became one of the fastest-growing (Institute of Medicine 1990) and most expensive areas of health care in the 1980s, generating huge profits for those with a stake in the industry (Weisner and Room 1984), substance abuse and dependence remained among the most prevalent psychiatric problems afflicting Americans. Thus, despite the growth of the substance abuse treatment industry, approximately 18 million Americans have problems related to their consumption of alcohol (National Institute on Alcohol Abuse and Alcoholism [NIAAA] 1990). Studies estimate that 7 to 14 percent of all drinkers experience symptoms of alcohol dependency (Hilton and Clark 1987), and 25 to 40 percent of the patients in general hospitals are being treated for medical complications related to their drinking, such as gastrointestinal, cardiovascular, and reproductive disorders (American Medical Association 1993). In addition, half of all homicides, suicides, and motor vehicle accidents are related to substance abuse (NIAAA 1990), and 5 percent of all deaths are alcohol related (Lewis 1990).

The economic costs are equally staggering. In 1988, the economic costs of alcohol-related problems alone were estimated to be $85.5 billion (Rice et al. 1990), and the NIAAA estimates that the economic costs will reach $150 billion in 1995 (1990).

As the gravity of the situation has intensified, the workplace has become one arena for reforming the rehabilitation of alcoholics and drug addicts. This has occurred for two reasons. The first is that some policymakers have identified the workplace as contributing significantly to the escalating costs of substance abuse treatment (Roman 1988). These policymakers argue that referral agents such as employee assistance counselors, doctors, psychologists, and social workers, who refer workers to treatment, have made too little effort to match clients with appropriate referrals; they have simply sent all workers suspected of being substance abusers to expensive inpatient treatment facilities. To counteract this trend and contain costs, the insurance industry has set up managed-care programs so it can monitor employees' use of their medical insurance for substance abuse treatment. In addition, policy experts have begun to devise clinical techniques for clinicians—whether they are EAP counselors, doctors, or social workers—to use in matching troubled employees with appropriate treatment programs (Institute of Medicine 1990).

The second reason the workplace has become a major focus for substance abuse treatment reform is the federal government's continuing war on drugs, which has encouraged employers to get tough on illicit drug users (Denenberg and Denenberg 1991). In addition, business coalitions, such as the Institute for a Drug-Free Workplace, claim that America is losing the war on drugs because the government, law enforcement officials, and schools are unable to win without the involvement of corporate America (de Bernardo 1988). Mark de Bernardo, the institute's executive director, claims that employers possess the most powerful weapon in this war—the paycheck—and they must wield it to keep employees drug-free. The institute recommends that employers take a variety of actions, including enforcing stringent drug-testing programs and tough EAP policies, to ensure that substance abusers are given only one chance at treatment.

A growing number of labor activists (McKay 1993; McCabe 1992) have begun to question many of the assumptions on which these reforms are based. They agree that inexpensive, high-quality programs are essential to prevent and treat workers with substance abuse problems. These activists also feel, however, that by further expanding the prevention and treatment infrastructure, which is grounded on hierarchical control, the problems will only be exacerbated. Specifically, they argue that reforms such as managed care and patient-treatment matching threaten to make the already bureaucratized and overprofessionalized medical system even more remote from, and unresponsive to, the real needs of substance-abusing workers. In particular, they fear that the precertification processes of managed-care providers are designed to discourage clients from using treatment services in order to save money for the insurance companies. They also fear that the individuals making precertification decisions for the managed care providers are not knowledgeable about addiction and its treatment. Additionally, they argue that company get-tough policies, such as those advocated by the Institute for a Drug-Free Workplace, discourage substance abusers from seeking assistance from their employers' EAPs because the workers are afraid of losing their jobs.

According to labor critics of the current treatment system, the process of reform must be rooted in a basic principle of communal voluntarism: the idea that workers can help one another by banding together. These critics claim that effective substance abuse and more general mental health programs must be firmly based in the communities that they serve and that the people who run the programs must keep a clear eye on their objective: helping those who suffer from substance abuse and dependence or other more general mental health problems.

Finally, the labor critics argue that, because of its historical commitment to these principles, labor is well positioned to lead such a reform effort, and they point to union-based member assistance programs (MAPs) as an important alternative to current employee assistance programs. In contrast to EAPs, which tend to emphasize the roles of supervisors and clinicians in helping troubled workers get treatment, MAPs emphasize the role of peer counselors—union members who volunteer their time to prevent substance abuse and help their co-workers who have substance abuse problems. MAPs are built around the idea of union members helping one another stay sober and "clean" (i.e., drug-free). This is not a new idea. It is the basis of craft unionism, and the existence of labor-based programs for assisting members is as old as the labor movement itself.

Labor's current effort to reform the substance abuse treatment system is being led by Labor Assistance Professionals (LAP), an organization established in 1991 to promote the development of peer-based MAPs within the labor movement. To date, there are LAP chapters in New York City, Boston, St. Louis, Fort Worth, Philadelphia, and San Francisco. According to LAP, the role of the workplace in the prevention and treatment of substance abuse must be redefined. LAP claims that the preoccupation with building a hierarchical professional treatment bureaucracy, grounded in the assumption that seeking help occurs only in response to managerial control, must be offset by a return to the basics of self-help and mutual aid, that is, to the spirit of communal voluntarism that underlies the American labor movement.

Because communities provide individuals a sense of belonging and a set of guidelines for how to behave, they are increasingly expected to play a critical role in the prevention and treatment of substance abuse problems (Cahalan 1991). Such a partnership is illustrated by the Center for Substance Abuse Prevention's current efforts to enlist work organizations in community efforts to combat substance abuse problems.

This bulletin describes the processes by which unions are implementing MAPs to prevent and treat alcohol and drug problems within the community of the workplace. Specifically, it focuses on three aspects of the process by which MAPs help union members: (1) how MAPs help prevent substance abuse at work, (2) how MAPs motivate members to seek help for their problems, and (3) how MAPs help union members maintain long-term abstinence. It is based on a study of MAPs in the airline and railroad industries, and it sets out a series of recommendations in the form of propositions that unions in other industries may want to use in developing their own programs. It is our hope that these propositions will also provide MAP administrators with a set of criteria for assessing their programs. Establishing such criteria is critical for understanding whether MAPs have achieved their goals of preventing substance abuse and whether those who require treatment have received it and maintained the ultimate long-term goal of sobriety and abstinence.

1

ORIGINS AND GOALS OF MEMBER ASSISTANCE PROGRAMS

Since the eighteenth century, the workplace has been a focus of the temperance movement, and since the nineteenth century, employers have played an active role in creating dry work organizations (Rumbarger 1989; Staudenmeier 1985). The relationship between temperance and work is complex because temperance serves both economic and symbolic functions; that is, the goal of the temperance movement is the construction of a highly disciplined society in which individuals exercise self-restraint and pursue their own interests to advance the common good (Lender and Martin 1987; Blocker 1989).

The temperance movement was the product of a changing society, one in transition from an agricultural- and craft-based economy to the new industrial order. Thus, some of the most avid supporters of temperance were prosperous master craftspeople who had expanded their businesses from small craft shops into factories, distancing themselves from their apprentices by becoming manager-owners and transforming their apprentices into wage laborers (Johnson 1978; Tyrell 1979). Temperance became a way of managing this transition process. It allowed the new manager-owners to challenge the predominant drinking patterns and to require that the workers exercise self-restraint. In the process, it symbolically underscored an important, early shift in the control of the work process, namely, that the manager-owners, and not the communities of craft workers, were responsible for controlling how the work would be performed.

During the colonial era, drinking on the job had been common because workers and employers alike had believed that alcoholic beverages such as beer and ale were necessary to preserve workers' health and provided them with the energy to perform their labors (Rorabaugh 1979). Master craft workers and their apprentices saw drinking as a way to create a sense of brotherhood, "a sort of secular sacrament, to seal the journeymen's social bonds within the customary artisanal regime" (Wilentz 1984:53–54), "a bond between men who lived, worked, and played together" (Johnson 1978:56).

Drinking as a ritual for constructing communal bonds at work began to come under attack in the latter part of the eighteenth century. Anthony Benezet, a wealthy Philadelphia Quaker, and Benjamin Rush, the father of American psychiatry, for example, argued that distilled spirits were destroying the moral order. They counseled farm owners to set an example for others by refraining from drinking ardent spirits and serving them to their farmhands. They assured the farm owners that, by setting an example for others, social order could be restored and that by refraining from supplying farm workers with ardent spirits, the crops would be harvested more quickly and with fewer disruptions. These arguments formed the basis of America's first temperance movement and successive ones as well.

By the 1820s, temperance leaders were pressing a full frontal attack on drinking customs in the workplace, initially by exhorting workers to abstain from drinking distilled spirits and eventually by pressing employers to prohibit the drinking of all alcoholic beverages both on and off the job (Rumbarger 1989). Eventually, a variety of employers adopted these reforms. During the 1820s, for instance, thousands of farmers adopted dry on-the-job policies for their farmhands, and by the 1840s, employers such as the Good Intent Stage Coach Line and the Utica and Schenectady railroads refused to hire anyone who drank (Staudenmeier 1985).

During the latter half of the nineteenth century, business owners intensified their efforts to root out workplace drinking. These efforts culminated in the 1890s in the formation of the Anti-Saloon League, which was among the temperance groups that pressured Congress to pass national prohibition (Rumbarger 1989; Blocker 1989).

Prohibition effectively removed drinking from most workplaces, and since its repeal, drinking on the job has not been a major issue for management and labor. In a few industries such as hospitality and construction, workers may still drink together on and off the job (Sonnenstuhl 1994), but in the majority of work organizations, most Americans today simply take for granted that on-the-job drinking is an unacceptable, even irrational, behavior because it causes accidents and decreases productivity (Gusfield 1987).

WORKERS' REACTIONS TO TEMPERANCE

Workers' reactions to temperance in the workplace have not been uniform. Responses have varied from outright hostility to the prohibitions against workplace drinking to a wholehearted embrace of temperance. These reactions reflect two intertwining routes unions have taken in their efforts to construct community in the face of the changing social relations at work and the prohibitions against on-the-job drinking by management.

Before temperance, drinking had been a way of uniting master craft workers and their apprentices; after temperance, workers drank in groups composed of workers only, in defiance of their employers' hierarchy-based attempts at control. Drinking thus created a sense of community and symbolized workers' resistance to the changing social relations at work (Clawson 1989). As Johnson (1978:60) notes: "An ancient bond between classes had become, within a very short time, an angry badge of working-class status."

In many occupations, drinking has remained a badge of working-class status and opposition to hierarchical control by management. Railroaders (Mannello and Seaman 1979), police (Van Maanen 1986), mariners (Molloy 1989), longshoremen (Mars 1987), and construction workers (Riemer 1979), for instance, still regard drinking as evidence of conformity to, rather than deviance from, occupational norms. Members of these occupations are *expected* to drink with one another on and off the job (Cosper 1979).

The persistence of such norms is epitomized by the sandhogs, a group of miners in New York City whose drinking culture can be traced to the birth of their union in the 1880s (Sonnenstuhl and Trice 1987; Sonnenstuhl 1994). For the sandhogs, drinking rituals are a means of constructing the union's occupational community. They create a boundary that separates members of the occupation from outsiders, and they symbolize the obligations members have to one another. Members are expected to drink with one another on and off the job, in defiance of management, and to cover up for one another's drinking. Drinking distinguishes members of the occupation from management, underscores members' obligations to protect one another, and creates strong solidarity among members. The sandhogs' drinking rituals have been remarkably persistent in that they are passed on from one generation of workers to the next, and because each generation experiences them as the means to achieving occupational survival.

Other nineteenth-century workers, however, embraced the notion of temperance: "For these men, temperance promoted the self-respect and self-discipline necessary to build a workers' community and a movement to resist the depredations of capital" (Blocker 1989:69). For instance, in the 1830s, the Boston Working Men's Protective Union required that its members be of "good moral character," be "capable of earning a livelihood," and "not use intoxicating drinks as a beverage" (quoted in Staudenmeier 1985:75). Similarly, during the latter half of the nineteenth century, labor leaders such as William H. Sylvis, head of the National Labor Union, and Terence V. Powderly, grand master of the Knights of Labor, characterized saloon keepers as social parasites who were sucking the lifeblood out of the working class and admonished their followers to lead temperate lives (Lender and Martin 1987). As one railway worker aptly put it, "As soon as a man has spent all his money for drink he becomes a slave of the corporation" (quoted in Blocker 1989:69).

Those workers and unions that encouraged temperance fell back on the craft tradition of mutual aid, communal voluntarism, and self-help as a way both to construct working-class solidarity (Clawson 1989) and to help workers with drinking problems. For instance, in the 1840s, six craft workers created the Washingtonians, the prototype for Alcoholics Anonymous (AA), to save workers from drunkenness and keep them sober (Blumberg 1991). Like AA, the Washingtonians maintained that the key to sobriety was for members to help others become sober. Throughout the rest of the nineteenth century, the Washingtonians served as the model for several other organizations dedicated to reforming drunkards, including the Sons of Temperance, the Good Templars, the Red, White, and Blue Ribbon Clubs, and the Catholic Total Temperance Union (Lender and Martin 1987; Blocker 1989).

In the twentieth century, unions have provided a variety of mental health and substance abuse services for their members. In the 1940s, for instance, the United Mine Workers, the International Ladies' Garment Workers, and the Teamsters operated psychiatric programs for their members (Ferguson and Fersing 1965). Also during this period, the Congress of Industrial Organizations, which merged with the American Federation of Labor to become the AFL-CIO, began its Community Services Department, which helped its affiliates develop peer counseling and referral programs for their members (Perlis 1980; Perlow 1979).

Since the 1940s, unions have promoted the development of alcoholism and employee assistance programs through such organizations as the National Council on Alcoholism (now called the National Council on Alcoholism and Drug Dependence) and the Association of Labor-Management Administrators and Consultants on Alcoholism (now the Employee Assistance Professionals Association) (Trice and Schonbrunn 1981; Steele 1989; Roman 1981).

Labor generally supported the development of EAPs, but it was also wary of them (Trice and Ritzer 1969; Roman 1981). Unions were afraid that management-sponsored mental health programs would diagnose union sympathizers as mentally ill and force them out of the workplace. At the same time, they worried that the EAPs would undermine their peer counseling programs, such as those advocated by the AFL-CIO's Community Services Department. Nevertheless, as Americans' belief in professionalism grew (Abbott 1988), unions wanted the benefits of "professional" treatment and bargained for such insurance coverage.

More recently, insurance companies have sought to restrict access to treatment, and many companies implemented tough substance abuse policies. In response, some labor activists, such as the members of LAP, began to question the efficacy of professional treatment and advocated a return to their traditions of self-help and mutual aid. The vehicle for undertaking this policy has been the MAP.

Today, many unions operate MAPs for the benefit of their members. These programs, like management-sponsored EAPs, help members with a wide range of family, mental health, and financial problems, but most focus on substance abuse because alcohol and other drug dependence are among the most prevalent disorders faced by workers and because workplace programs are the most effective means of treating substance abuse and chemical dependence (Sonnenstuhl and Trice 1990; Roman 1988). MAPs encourage union members to seek help for their problems, refer troubled members to community agencies for treatment, and provide follow-up to ensure successful treatment.

MAPS AND COMMUNAL CONTROL

One reason MAPs have the potential to be so effective at reducing substance abuse is that, unlike EAPs, they exercise communal or normative control over union members (Etzioni 1961; Sonnenstuhl and Trice 1990). Peers rather than supervisors promote conformity by defining, responding to, and controlling what is considered deviant behavior (Parsons 1951; Pitts 1961; Horwitz 1990). Specifically, MAPs define certain behavior, such as alcohol or drug use, as unacceptable because it impairs job performance. Further, they promote conformity to workplace norms, such as maintaining performance standards, by referring substance abusers to treatment, including AA and inpatient and outpatient counseling, and by providing them long-term workplace support.

The primary goals of an MAP are to change the behavior of substance abusers and repair the bonds between them and family members, coworkers, and others that have been disrupted by the abusers' unacceptable behavior (Horwitz 1990). MAPs provide workers and their colleagues a mechanism for accounting for these individuals' impairment and a method for restoring them to full health and reintegrating them into their work groups.

Today's MAPs are not prohibitionist; they do not seek to prohibit the use of alcohol and other drugs in American society. Rather, MAPs are temperance organizations in that they urge workers to drink responsibly and to refrain from the use of illicit drugs. They are thus mechanisms for transforming cultures defined by their drinking into cultures that advocate sobriety.

Contemporary MAPs promote drug-free workplaces by emphasizing that the use of alcohol, other drugs, or both on the job is a violation of union and occupational norms and by defining off-the-job use of alcohol and other drugs that impairs job performance as unacceptable. The peer counselors in MAPs also promote this message. In responding to union members who violate drug- and alcohol-related norms, for example, a peer counselor initially emphasizes what is acceptable behavior, urges the workers to comply voluntarily with occupational norms before their supervisors take disciplinary action, and finally offers referrals to workers who cannot comply with the norms because they suffer from alcoholism or drug addiction.

Peer counselors use a combination of positive and negative tactics to motivate co-workers to stop drinking and using drugs at work, to seek therapeutic help for personal problems that adversely affect their job performance, and to follow treatment recommendations to abstain from using alcohol or other drugs. Positive tactics include praising coworkers who comply with occupational norms, telling them they are valued members of the occupational community, and underscoring the union's commitment to help members who are unable to comply with norms because they suffer from alcoholism or addiction. Negative tactics range from the relatively benign, such as providing feedback to coworkers who do not comply with expectations, to the extremely harsh, including reminding co-workers that if the undesirable behavior continues, management will probably take action and the union may not be able to do anything to prevent the consequences.

Most co-workers will conform to occupational norms because they value their union membership and fear being excluded from the group (Braithwaite 1989; Horwitz 1990). They want to be thought of as good union members and do not want their co-workers to think ill of them. They will readily comply when peers simply restate group expectations.

Other co-workers respond especially well to economic incentives; that is, they may be resistant to moral suasion but respond to actions that threaten to stop their paychecks, most notably the threat of discipline by their supervisors. In these cases, there is also the threat of being excluded from the group, but it stems from their supervisors' willingness to take disciplinary action. Experts in EAPs (Trice and Roman 1978) regard the threat of disciplinary action as especially effective in overcoming denial and motivating alcoholic and drug-addicted workers to seek therapeutic help.

The ultimate goal of an MAP is to create a working environment in which union members exercise self-control over their behavior: an environment in which workers take for granted that drinking and using drugs at work are unacceptable and act accordingly, and an environment in which those who suffer from substance abuse problems will receive help for their illnesses.

2

MAPS IN THE TRANSPORTATION INDUSTRY

Unlike many other studies of health-related workplace intervention programs, our study of MAPs did not evaluate program outcomes. Rather, it focused on the implementation process. Our reasons for this were straightforward. A health-related workplace intervention program cannot be expected either to prevent substance abuse or to achieve high rates of abstinence among treated workers unless fully implemented (Beyer and Trice 1978). We approached our study with the assumption that, like any intervention based on communal voluntarism, MAPs must be fully implemented before they can achieve their objectives. Therefore, we wanted to identify those factors critical to the effective design and implementation of MAPs. We sought to do so by investigating the processes by which union members actually implement programs: What did they do to implement their programs? What barriers to implementation have they experienced? What have they done to overcome them? What do they feel is working or not working? In addition a primary goal in this investigation was to identify the issues union members interested in starting and institutionalizing a member assistance program need to consider. Thus, we sought to generate insights about both the rules and responsibilities of union members interested in establishing and maintaining an MAP, and the process that results in a union member seeking treatment from an MAP.

We are indebted to Valerie Kennedy, who collected field data on Operation:RedBlock. A fuller description of the CSXT's Operation:RedBlock is available in Kennedy and Sonnenstuhl, 1992.

We have used a study design that is similar to that of "action science" (Argyris, Putnam, and McLain 1985), and the propositions we have generated are similar to those generated in an "action theory." As Argyris and his colleagues put it, action science is based on the idea that the social sciences should not only describe the present but challenge the status quo and "generate liberating alternatives." Like conventional social science, action science results in solid and systematic social theory, grounded in hard data and subject to public and empirical testing. But unlike conventional social science, the goal of action science is not only to describe and explain phenomena but to bring about change.

Proponents of action science start with the assumption that those involved in doing rarely reflect on either the ends they are trying to achieve or on the links between the means to those ends and the ends themselves. Argyris and his colleagues believe that it is up to researchers to break through these "theories in use" and identify the propositions that emerge from the action context.

To the extent that action science requires the generation of propositions, to be tested in an ongoing intervention, it requires the adoption of a constant-comparison methodology similar to the one proposed by Glaser and Strauss (1967; Strauss 1987). We used the constant-comparison method in our study precisely because the focus was on generating theories, not on testing them. The constant-comparison method was designed to develop rich descriptions of social phenomena and to generate hypotheses and theories about them.

Briefly, the constant-comparison method worked in our study as follows. First, we asked our subjects a series of questions: How did your MAP get started, and how has it changed? What roles have the union and management played in the program as it has evolved? What roles have supervisors and peer counselors played in the program as it has evolved?

While we observed, interviewed, and wrote up our field notes, we looked for incidents bearing on these questions, including specific references in our interviews, direct observations from our field notes, and written evidence in the archival data. In comparing one incident with another, salient categories began to emerge. For instance, joint action by supervisors and peer counselors emerged as an explanation for why some workers sought help from an MAP. Archival data confirmed that supervisors and peer counselors engage in joint actions to motivate troubled workers to seek help. Joint action, then, was assumed to be a salient category for understanding the role of labor-management cooperation in the implementation and maintenance of MAPs.

We also wanted to know the properties of joint actions: What happens in joint actions? Who initiates joint actions and under what circumstances? How do joint actions prompt troubled co-workers to seek help? In pursuing the answers to such questions, we collected more data and made comparisons with more incidents. Slowly, a detailed description of, and hypotheses about, joint actions emerged.

Next, we compared MAPs to see whether our descriptions and hypotheses held in these cases as well. When they did not fit, we modified the hypotheses accordingly. The underlying goal of this process is replication (Yin 1984); cases that confirm the existence of relationships enhance confidence in the validity of the relationships (Eisenhardt 1989). To increase the internal validity and generalizability of our emergent theory, we also attempted to integrate it with existing literature (Eisenhardt 1989; Denzin 1986).

All the coded data—interviews, observations, and archival material— were analyzed with a prolog-based system called AQUAD 3.1 that is used to generate theory from qualitative data (Huber 1991). The analysis provided us the means both to refine our hypotheses and to assess the degree to which our emerging model was empirically sound.

We used this methodology to examine three MAPs. The first program was established by the Association of Flight Attendants and is referred to as the AFA EAP. The other two programs, both called Operation:Red-Block, are used in the railroad industry, one at CSX Transportation (CSXT) and the other at Amtrak.

AFA EAP

The Association of Flight Attendants (AFL-CIO) represents approximately thirty-three thousand flight attendants employed by eighteen carriers, including United, USAir, Hawaiian, Alaska, Tower, and Midway. The association's employee assistance program (AFA EAP) was established in 1980.

Originally supported by a grant from the National Institute of Alcohol Abuse and Alcoholism, the proposed EAP was to be administered jointly by the AFA and the managements of the eighteen carriers with AFA members. This plan was never carried out, however, because the managements of the carriers demanded that the AFA adopt only a limited role in referral, which the AFA refused to do, and the carriers preferred to develop EAPs to serve not only flight attendants but all airline employees. Thus, within a year after the AFA EAP was started, the union became fully responsible for operating it. Then, when the NIAAA funding period ended, the union assumed full financial responsibility for the program.

The goal of the AFA EAP is to help flight attendants deal with a wide range of personal problems, including chemical dependency, marital and family difficulties, stress, and eating disorders. Much of the success of the program is due to the network of active flight attendants who volunteer their time and energy to act as peer counselors. None of these counselors is paid for EAP work, and they all do it in addition to their regular jobs. Depending on case loads and circumstances, the counselors may spend considerable time working for the EAP.

The director of the EAP and her staff at AFA headquarters train the peer counselors to assume both passive and active peer counseling and crisis roles. In their passive role, the peer counselors provide information to troubled flight attendants when solicited; that is, they wait for coworkers to ask for help. The counselors then assess their colleagues' problems and refer them to community agencies or self-help groups for assistance.

In their active role, the peer counselors seek out troubled colleagues and provide them with unsolicited recommendations about their problem behavior; that is, they confront them with evidence of their problems and encourage them to accept help before these problems get out of hand. Various events, including direct observations of a coworker, reports from other employees about a coworker's job behavior, and requests from supervisors having trouble with an employee, can prompt a peer counselor to confront a worker with his or her need for help. In all cases, the peer counselor's objective remains the same: to help the troubled flight attendant and his or her family members resolve their behavioral problems.

At each domicile or home base, the peer counselors are organized into a local AFA EAP committee, which is part of the union local's operating structure. This committee is responsible for day-to-day program operations, including working with other union committees (e.g., grievance, health and safety, professional standards), publicizing the services of the EAP to new flight attendants and the general membership, providing ongoing training for new peer counselors, developing community resources, and counseling troubled flight attendants. The committee is also responsible for reporting utilization and other case-related data to the AFA's national EAP office and, through the carrier's EAP steering committee, for coordinating activities with other local EAP committees that service flight attendants who work for the same carrier in other cities. EAP steering committees meet once or twice a year depending on the carrier, and they include the chairs of all the carrier's EAP committees.

The president of the local appoints the chair of the local EAP committee on the recommendation of the previous chair, current committee members, or both. Only rarely is this appointment influenced by local union politics. The chair is responsible for recruiting new committee members.

Flight attendants recovering from alcoholism and other addictions make ideal peer counselors because they have experiential knowledge of the problems for which they are providing help. The majority of the peer counselors, however, are not recovering from alcoholism or other addictions. Rather, they are simply union members committed to helping other flight attendants solve their problems. Many become peer counselors because they have been helped by the program. Some become counselors as a way to get involved in the union, others because they are interested in a mental health career in the future.

Local chairs have several specific responsibilities. First, although most peer counselors have their own management contacts, the chair is responsible for maintaining the committee's relations with management. Second, the chair is responsible for communicating with the union's airline-wide EAP director (a part-time position in the unions at the larger airlines such as United) and with the union's national EAP office. Third, the chair is responsible for ensuring that unionwide EAP policies, such as the right to confidentiality for all workers seeking help through the EAP, are followed and that monthly activity reports are filed with the national EAP office. Fourth, and finally, the chair assigns new cases to peer counselors. Veteran counselors receive most of their cases directly from the field, based on their good reputations, but new counselors, at least initially, rely on the chair for case assignments. Assignments tend to become specialized as counselors either develop a recognized field of expertise, such as eating disorders or substance abuse, or they focus on a particular sector of the flight attendant community, such as gays, blacks, or seniors.

OPERATION:REDBLOCK

Within the railroad industry, the term *redblock* refers to the signal light telling locomotive engineers to stop their trains because of potential dangers ahead. The program Operation:RedBlock derives its name from this signal. The primary goal of Operation:RedBlock is to prevent drinking and drugging in the railroad industry. As mentioned earlier, a drinking culture has existed among railroaders since the inception of the industry in the early nineteenth century, and the railroads were early supporters of the temperance movement (Staudenmeier 1985). Since the 1880s, management has attempted to eliminate drinking on the job by enforcing Operating Rule G, which states that anyone drinking on company property, in possession of intoxicants on company property, or reporting to work under the influence of alcohol is subject to summary discharge. To strengthen Rule G, management has strived to enforce Operating Rule E, which requires co-workers to report infractions of Rule G or be subject to termination.

To management's chagrin, Rules G and E have not deterred railroaders from drinking or using drugs. Rather, they have contributed to strengthening the drinking culture by encouraging workers to cover up for one another's drinking to protect one another's jobs (Mannello and Seaman 1979).

Although the railroads were early adopters of EAPs (Hitchcock and Sanders 1976), these programs, like Rules G and E, were ineffective at curtailing drinking in the industry (Mannello and Seaman 1979). Although the programs were effective at helping workers who sought assistance from them, they did not reach those workers with the most extreme cases of alcoholism and other addictions because their co-workers continued to cover for them.

T. A. Mannello and F. J. Seaman, who conducted a study of railroad EAPs, published their findings in 1978 in what has come to be known as the REAP report. They concluded that in direct violation of Rule G and, in spite of the existence of a twenty-year-old management-based program, 23 percent of railroad operating personnel were "problem drinkers" and 5 percent reported to work "very drunk" or became "very drunk" on duty at least once in the study year. In addition, they concluded that, because substance abusers feared dismissal, most Rule G violations went unreported and few problem drinkers ever received the assistance they needed from the EAP.

The release of the REAP report caused quite a stir in the railroad industry because it implied that, on any given day, many railroaders were drinking and using drugs. Both management and labor perceived the report as stigmatizing the industry. Management worried that the report would further discourage travelers accustomed to traveling by car, plane, and bus, and dissuade companies that were accustomed to moving their products by truck from using the trains. Likewise, many railroaders who were fed up with risking their lives and jobs to protect co-workers who drank and used drugs felt that something had to be done to save their reputations as decent and hard working while protecting co-workers' lives and jobs. Consequently, both labor and management sought changes in the EAP, with the general goal of enhancing safety on the rails and promoting a more positive image of the industry and its workers.

In 1980, the idea for Operation:RedBlock was proposed by Jimmy Dargon, a Union Pacific Railroad brakeman in Kansas. His idea was simple. Since management had failed to change the railroaders' drinking and drug-using culture by enforcing Rules G and E, the unions would have to change that culture themselves. To do so effectively required some guarantees from management that workers who were in violation of Rule G would be treated rather than discharged summarily. Working with the Brotherhood of Locomotive Engineers (BLE) and the United Transportation Union (UTU), the Union Pacific was the first railroad to adopt Operation:RedBlock.

Operation:RedBlock has developed several mechanisms for ensuring that workers receive help rather than discipline for violating Rule G. These are the Rule G By-Pass Agreement, the companion agreement, and procedures for "marking off" RedBlock.

According to the Rule G By-Pass Agreement, an employee in violation of Rule G can seek treatment from the EAP rather than face discharge. In lieu of being disciplined, the employee can go to an EAP counselor, comply with his or her advice, and return to active duty when the counselor certifies the employee is able to do so. The companion agreement permits managers and supervisors to refer workers in violation of Rule G to the EAP for treatment. As in the By-Pass Agreement, the employee is expected to comply with the EAP counselor's recommendations and upon successful completion of treatment the employee is returned to active duty.

Workers who have been drinking or drugging may also mark off RedBlock. The mark-off is a set of procedures for keeping employees under the influence of alcohol and other drugs off the railroad. Mark-offs are of two types. First, workers who have been drinking or drugging and are called to duty may mark themselves off from duty that day without any penalty. This is treated as an excused absence. Alternatively, an employee may report to work and be under the influence. In this case, he or she may also mark himself or herself off duty and be excused. In addition, if the worker who is under the influence does not mark himself off, his co-workers may mark him off and send him home.

After a worker either marks himself off or is marked-off by his co-workers, the RedBlock committee, which is made up of union members, talks to the worker to determine whether he is a substance abuser and requires treatment or whether there is another explanation for why he was in violation of Rule G (e.g., he was unexpectedly called for duty while attending his daughter's wedding). If the worker needs treatment, the committee members refer him to the company's EAP; if the worker has been called to duty unexpectedly, they will praise him for marking off and not endangering everyone's lives and warn him to be careful next time.

Since its adoption at Union Pacific, Operation:RedBlock programs have been developed at other railroads. Still, although preliminary results from at least one study (Eichler et al. 1988) are encouraging, the list of railroads with RedBlock programs is surprisingly short. Among the most successful are those at CSX Transportation and Amtrak.

CSXT

CSX Transportation is a freight railroad that serves the eastern part of the United States. It was formed after the merger of the Chessie System Railroads and the Family Lines Railroads in 1981.

The Chessie System Railroads had been a pioneer in the use of Operation:RedBlock as a result of its participation in the REAP study in the late 1970s. At that time, Chessie's management, which had a reputation for taking care of its workers, had recognized that its EAP was not reaching everyone who needed help. In 1983, Chessie adopted a system-wide Rule G By-Pass Agreement, and in 1984, at the suggestion of a BLE local chairman, it began investigating the adoption of the Operation:RedBlock program. Consequently, when the United Transportation Union (UTU) approached the railroad about the possibility of adopting the Union Pacific's innovative Operation:RedBlock program, Chessie's management was receptive. In 1984, Chessie's management, the Chessie EAP, the UTU, and the BLE formally agreed to start Operation:RedBlock.

Today, Operation:RedBlock exists throughout CSXT. The program was originally implemented under the auspices of the company's EAP, but it is now under the direction of CSXT's labor-management program. Both CSXT's management and its unions point to Operation:RedBlock as an example of what labor and management cooperation can accomplish.

One reason often given for putting Operation:RedBlock under the labor-management program is to distinguish it from the company EAP. Whereas CSXT railroaders regard the EAP with some suspicion as a management program, they regard RedBlock as a union program whose mission is to save workers' lives. Indeed, before Operation:RedBlock, many railroaders felt uncomfortable seeking help from the company EAP, and their co-workers felt unable to provide them with the help they needed.

Management supports Operation:RedBlock financially, but the unions run the program. At the corporate level, there are two full-time coordinators. The first two unionists who held these positions were locomotive engineers and chairmen of their union locals, one from the UTU, the other from the BLE. In 1992, the coordinator from the BLE returned to his former engineering job. He was replaced with a captain of a UTU RedBlock team. The coordinators remain active union leaders and are on temporary assignment with Operation:RedBlock.

The primary responsibilities of the coordinators have been to establish Operation:RedBlock committees at every CSXT terminal and to teach committee members how to train CSXT employees to use the mark-off procedures. Committee members have learned these skills through a variety of training programs. Two rounds of training have been held at each site; these focused on how to set up a committee, conduct an education program, and perform the required intervention following mark-offs. A third round of training that covers the basics of substance abuse and how to motivate substance abusers to accept treatment is in process. In addition, Operation:RedBlock holds periodic division meetings and an annual meeting to develop program strategy and members' skills.

The RedBlock committee at each terminal is composed of a team captain and several volunteers. According to the program's coordinators, the ideal committee includes both recovering alcoholics and addicts as well as social drinkers and abstainers. All the committee members are unpaid volunteers who are committed to creating a safe working environment by keeping alcohol and other drugs off the railroads and helping their co-workers deal with substance abuse problems.

Each committee is entirely responsible for developing its own educational programs. Some committees have distributed wallet cards instructing co-workers on the mark-off procedures; others have given out hats and pens with the RedBlock logo that serve as reminders of the procedures. Committees have also organized a variety of activities, including picnics, visits to the zoo, and raffles, to promote awareness of RedBlock and to develop esprit de corps among the railroaders and their families.

The overall thrust of Operation:RedBlock has been to develop a close working relationship with CSXT's EAP. That is, the Operation:RedBlock teams have generally sought to identify substance abusers and work with the EAP to ensure that they receive appropriate treatment and long-term support for maintaining their sobriety. As some committee members have gained experience in their Operation:RedBlock roles, however, a few have begun to consider the possibility of developing skills such as those required of the peer counselors in the AFA EAP.

Amtrak

In contrast to CSXT, the National Railroad Passenger Corporation, commonly known as Amtrak, is supported by Congress. Amtrak had always been a tough employer with respect to substance abusers, relying heavily on enforcement of Rule G to rid its roads of alcohol and drugs. Consequently, it was somewhat reluctant to adopt Operation:RedBlock until its effectiveness had been proven. Management's stance changed, however, after Congress undertook hearings on a train crash in Chase, Maryland. A Conrail engineer, who was high on drugs, failed to obey a signal and collided with an Amtrak train. During the congressional hearings it was suggested that having a program such as Operation: RedBlock might prevent future drug-related accidents. Amtrak began its RedBlock program in 1988.

Before implementing RedBlock, Amtrak's EAP director and its coordinator for the program spent several months consulting with the staff of Union Pacific and CSXT's programs. Consequently, Amtrak's program bears many similarities to CSXT's, including the use of mark-off agreements, a corporate-level coordinator and staff who are responsible for program implementation, and local RedBlock committees composed of volunteers charged with educating their co-workers about the mark-off procedures and referring those in need of treatment to the company EAP.

Amtrak's program differs from CSXT's, however, in several significant ways. First, at the time of the study, Operation:RedBlock at Amtrak was under the supervision of its EAP. In 1994, however, the program was moved out from under EAP and placed under the company's safety program. While the program was under the direct supervision of the EAP, there was no clear division between the two programs. Consequently, some employees were confused about whether the program was sponsored by management or the union.

Second, while both programs put primary responsibility on local RedBlock teams for handling all mark-offs, at Amtrak, mark-offs may also be reported to the coordinators by phoning an 800 number. Although these calls are generally referred back to the local team captains, the senior coordinator and his staff may also handle them.

Third, unlike the CSXT program, the one at Amtrak has only recently completed the first phase of implementation: recruitment of RedBlock committee members and initial training. Thus, the coordinators of CSXT's Operation:RedBlock can confidently say that every employee knows about the program and its mark-off provisions. In contrast, on Amtrak, there are wide variations in employees' knowledge about the program and its procedures because the program has not yet been fully implemented.

Fourth, at both CSXT and Amtrak, participation in Operation:Red-Block is voluntary for both unions and their members. On CSXT, the BLE, the UTU, and the Brotherhood of Railroad Signalmen (BRS) are active participants in the program. Thus, all members of the train crews are represented in the program. At Amtrak, thirteen unions represent a wide range of workers, including members of the train crew, on-board services, and maintenance functions. This means that the program is more complex than at CSXT. For instance, while mark-offs all follow the same procedures at CSXT, they vary according to craft at Amtrak. At the same time, the Operation:RedBlock program at Amtrak is providing these unions with a sense of unity which they have not experienced in the past.

COMPARISON OF THE THREE PROGRAMS

In all three programs, peer counselors are trained to help co-workers suffering from substance abuse and other problems get the assistance they need. Similarly, they are trained to help recovering co-workers return to work and, in the case of those suffering from substance abuse problems, maintain long-term abstinence. Finally, the counselors in all three programs serve as informal agents of cultural change. To varying degrees, all three occupational communities have cultures that have supported substance abuse in the past. For instance, in the past, flight attendants often saw drinking as a way of coping with work stress, and railroaders saw drinking on the job as a mark of their solidarity against management. Thus, by redefining drinking and using drugs on the job as deviant, peer counselors serve as the front line in a union-based substance abuse prevention effort.

The programs also differ in several ways. One important difference is their focus. The two programs at the railroads emphasize the prevention of substance abuse. They rely on company-run EAPs to provide diagnosis, referral, and follow-up. In contrast, the AFA EAP focuses on a variety of problems, and it both refers workers to care within the community and provides follow-up services to ensure that the problems have been properly treated and that the workers are recovering.

In pointing out these differences, we do not mean to suggest that the volunteers in the Operation:RedBlock programs are unconcerned with providing services to workers with problems other than substance abuse or that the AFA EAP is unconcerned with preventing substance abuse. Rather, the differences reflect the different needs of the two occupational communities. Operation:RedBlock was established to meet the needs of a predominantly male workforce with a well-developed substance abuse culture, which had been in existence since the beginning of railroading. In contrast, most of the workers the AFA EAP serves are women who, unlike men, have not traditionally built a sense of communal solidarity around drinking and drugging. Rather, they have built solidarity around helping one another with their personal problems. Thus, women are generally more open than men are about their personal problems and more willing to seek help from mental health services than men are (Horwitz 1990). The AFA EAP reflects this different tradition.

Second, the programs vary in their sources of financial support. The AFA EAP receives all its financial support from the union. In contrast, both the CSXT and Amtrak Operation:RedBlock programs receive a great deal of financial support from management, as well as from union members who volunteer their time and energy to make the program work. As we shall see, these differences affect the maintenance of MAPs over the long term.

Third, the paid staff in the three programs have different backgrounds. In the AFA EAP, the staff at the national headquarters are professionals. In contrast, Operation:RedBlock's national staff are railroaders who do not have clinical experience. There is little difference, however, in the primary consultative roles of these staff members; that is, their function in all the programs is to ensure that the peer counselors have the resources to perform their crucial roles.

Fourth, the programs vary in the degree to which they have been implemented. This variation is a function of several factors: (1) when the programs were developed, (2) when each organization adopted the program, and (3) the resources each organization has contributed to the process of implementation. The AFA EAP, for instance, was started more than a decade ago. Since then, the program has expanded its focus from substance abuse to broad-brush mental health issues. In contrast, the Operation:RedBlock programs were started relatively recently, primarily in response to a specific need to change the drinking culture on the railroads. This is particularly the case at Amtrak, where RedBlock has only recently been implemented.

STUDY DATA

In conducting our research, we spent months in the field following a wide variety of railroad personnel from one property to the next and meeting flight attendants in airport lounges from Los Angeles to Boston and from Seattle to Atlanta. We interviewed sixty-six flight attendants, AFA union leaders, in-flight supervisors, and base managers, as well as a similar number of railroad employees and managers, ranging from yard managers to top executives. We also conducted a dozen focus group interviews (both on-site and at our offices at Cornell University) and attended numerous training programs for participants in the AFA, CSXT, and Amtrak programs.

Our efforts left us with hundreds of hours of taped interviews, which were then transformed into thousands of pages of transcripts. These transcripts were then coded and analyzed using the software package described earlier.

In the following pages, we present several propositions that were generated from our interviews, observations, and archival data. These propositions are intended to serve as guidelines for unions that are starting MAPs for the first time or restructuring existing ones. Following these guidelines will help ensure that the MAP will be as successful as possible.

3

ESTABLISHING AND MAINTAINING AN MAP

A spirit of communal voluntarism is essential if an MAP is to be successful. As some LAP members have said, "Who is better equipped than a plumber to help a plumber, and who is better equipped than a professor to help a professor?"

Communal voluntarism is the essential source of MAPs' effectiveness in reaching chemically dependent workers and helping them achieve long-term sobriety. The ethic of communal voluntarism is also the basis for the claim of advocates of MAPs that they can make better use of resources than EAPs. In short, it is essential that an MAP have a well-established ethic of communal voluntarism from its inception and that union members strive to maintain it.

Several factors are important in maintaining this spirit and ensuring program success. Among those we identified were a concern with meeting the needs of union members, a nondisciplinary philosophy, the use of teams of peer counselors, and program autonomy. In this chapter, we present several propositions concerning the effects of these and other variables on the successful establishment and maintenance of an MAP.

IMPLEMENTING AND STRUCTURING AN MAP

In establishing an MAP, union members must address two primary issues. The first has to do with the process of implementation, and the second has to do with the program's administrative structure. Our research generated several propositions concerning both issues.

Proposition 3.1: Successful implementation of an MAP requires both the support of the union leadership and the involvement of members at the grassroots level.

Nothing is more indicative of the communal voluntaristic nature of MAPs than the way they are initiated. MAPs emerge in reaction to the defined needs of workers. Sometimes the union members identify this need, sometimes the union leadership. We found that MAPs were most successful when both the union leaders and the grassroots members supported them from the start. For example, the idea for Operation:RedBlock came from a UTU brakeman who recognized the need to change the railroaders' substance abuse culture. Similarly, a group of recovering flight attendants put pressure on the leadership of the AFA to address what they saw as a deepening problem with the members' mental well-being. One flight attendant told us:

> We finally just hit our limits in terms of how much we could be pushed around and how much stress we could live with and deny. When the eighties came along—with the opening of all the Pandora boxes—we realized that if anybody's got problems, it's us! At a certain point, conditions got to the point where our people just started saying, "No! We're in pain and if you, management, aren't going to recognize it and deal with it, we will!"

This group called on the union to establish an EAP to help troubled flight attendants, or TFAs. One of the members of that group recalled that

> it was in the late seventies when we started to realize the need. People were interested in it because the problems were all too clear and could no longer be denied. We had people—frankly, they were recovering individuals—that weren't terribly enamored with the way they were treated throughout their recovery process. And I think that gave them incentive to push to establish this kind of program and then to help build it. Their own experiences gave them the incentive to make sure that whatever was not comfortable for them would be addressed by an EAP and that the policies that worked against their recovery would never be able to take their toll on another flight attendant without the union first trying to do something about it.

Another flight attendant said that the union finally decided to do something about the growing problem of the employees' mental well-being in general, and substance abuse in particular, when a recovering flight attendant made a personal plea to the union's board of directors:

The idea for the EAP came about when this woman went to AFA's board of directors meeting and told her story. She told her story like an alcoholic telling a story, saying that there was a need for a program. As a result, . . . they decided that something needed to be done.

In contrast, the decision to start an MAP at Amtrak came from the top down, in response to congressional pressure, and this top-down implementation process may be the underlying cause of some of the tensions in the program today. Rather than the unions initiating the program, top management initiated it, perhaps leaving an impression that Operation:RedBlock was intended to discipline workers rather than help them.

Proposition 3.2: Volunteers in successful MAPs have a strong desire to enhance their co-workers' emotional and mental well-being.

We found that successful MAP teams and committees were composed of individuals who had a profound sense of calling; that is, they felt a deep sense of obligation to aid their co-workers in need. For some, this calling emerged from their own experiences in recovery. For others, it emerged from their sense of responsibility and connection to their community. Indeed, voluntaristic communalism, which the labor movement has often equated with fraternalism and solidarity, is the underlying philosophy of Alcoholics Anonymous and other self-help groups. Thus, as in AA, MAP peer counselors often refer to the "need to give something back" as the underlying reason they volunteer their time to an MAP.

MAPs extend the sense of responsibility workers feel for one another. In the process, they also reinvigorate the attitude among unions that they have an obligation to their members that goes beyond typical bread-and-butter issues. We found that MAPs forced unions, especially those characterized for years by machismo indifference, to redefine their priorities. In the railroad industry, for instance, Operation:Red-Block was responsible for pushing the brotherhoods to return to their mutual aid roots. One Operation:RedBlock activist told us:

I see this program growing into a labor movement. . . . We have a group of people that have realized they have an effect on the workplace; they have an effect on people's lives. A lot of people get a lot of strokes out of helping people. Probably the best eulogy you could ever get is, "In life, the guy helped somebody along the way!" So I see this as something more than a program; it's a process of getting people reinvolved in labor . . . an opportunity to make people understand that being a union member gives you some responsibilities as well as a right to work on this railroad.

The most successful MAP teams and committees made it clear that part of their mission was the enhancement of the *overall* well-being of their members; they did not confuse this mission with other union-specific concerns, such as job security and due process. As several MAP activists involved in both the AFA and CSXT programs told us, "Our job is no less than to save lives." Similarly, at each Amtrak Operation:Red-Block training, the coordinators tell members, "We are our Brothers' Keepers; the only obligation we have to one another is to tell the truth."

In discussing MAP intervention activities with AFA EAP peer counselors, we learned of many cases in which counselors had to choose between an action aimed at getting an individual to accept his or her need for help and an action that would have protected the individual's job but, at its core, was enabling. Committees whose peer counselors understood and identified with the goal of enhancing members' overall well-being were generally more able to get troubled members to seek help and initiate the process of long-term recovery. Thus, when one of the AFA's most effective peer counselors was faced with the choice of helping a co-worker get through a flight, thus enabling her, or helping her get into treatment, the choice was clear, although she was risking both their jobs by encouraging the co-worker to walk off the job after checking in for the flight without informing the supervisor of the reason.

> I said [to my co-worker], "This is your job. You've got to be honest with me. I want to help you, but you have to tell me the truth." And I'm just looking at her. And then she says, "Yeah, I've been drinking." So I say, "When did you drink?" She says, "Twenty minutes ago." And she just checked in for a flight? Now, I can't let her go on a flight. I can't do that, right? I mean in every way she couldn't go. So, I came out and said, "Okay, I'm going to try and get you out of here. So, let me just see what I can do. I've got to try to get you out of here."

Proposition 3.3: MAPs are most successful when their goals are flexible and can be adjusted to meet the particular needs of the membership base.

An MAP's mission statement should be broad, to allow the MAP to pursue diverse goals. Given the underlying spirit of communal voluntarism, a program should not be exclusionary. For instance, from the beginning, the Operation:RedBlock teams at both CSXT and Amtrak have sought to ensure that the program was inclusive by including social drinkers as well as recovering alcoholics as team members. The CSXT coordinators and some team captains believe that the Union Pacific MAP failed because its focus was too narrow. The comments of one CSXT coordinator reflect this sentiment:

> On another division . . . a group of people gained control and took the approach of the Union Pacific. They had the ones [AAs who were RedBlock team members] who were superactive. . . . They scared off a lot of people; they intimidated a lot of people. They confronted a lot of people who more than likely didn't need to be confronted or, if they did, it needed to be done in a different manner.

To avoid creating a feeling of exclusion, the Operation:RedBlock teams at both CSXT and Amtrak have tried to include union members who are abstainers, social drinkers, and recovering alcoholics. In addition, the message conveyed at all program-related training is that the MAP is for everyone, since saving someone's life, family, and job is everyone's concern.

Recently, the programs at CSXT and Amtrak have begun to consider problems other than substance abuse as within their purview. This evolution has occurred as the MAP team members have helped substance abusers deal with related problems. As one CSXT coordinator said:

> With Operation:RedBlock, we have not only started a prevention and intervention program, we have also enhanced the [company's] employee assistance program by making it more visible, [by helping] people see that these programs are not just for alcohol and drug problems but are there for family problems, marital, financial, whatever the case may be.

Similarly, although originally suggested as an alcoholism program by the recovering flight attendants, AFA established it as a broad-based mental health program by the mid-1980s.

Proposition 3.4: The more committed an MAP is to a nondisciplinary philosophy, the more successful it will be in achieving its potential.

Successful MAPs emphasize their nondisciplinary nature. They underscore that union members never put their jobs at risk when they seek help through the program. As the director of Amtrak's Operation:Red-Block stated, "The sole intent of the RedBlock committees is to create and protect an unobstructed pathway to treatment resources by either self-admission or co-worker–induced referral."

EAPs are built around the disciplinary process, which they use as a lever for overcoming the psychodynamics of denial that characterize alcoholism and other addictions (Sonnenstuhl and Trice 1990; Roman 1988). Consequently, no matter how often EAPs tell employees that they won't be punished for seeking help, some will continue to feel that in going to the program they are exposing themselves to disciplinary action. Our findings indicate that it is thus important for MAPs to distinguish themselves from management-run EAPs.

The CSXT Operation:RedBlock teams initially had a great deal of difficulty differentiating their program from the company's EAP, because the RedBlock teams referred alcoholic workers to the management-run program. The teams had to work very hard at clarifying that their role is to save jobs, not jeopardize them. One coordinator summarized this view:

You've got a few people out there you can talk to and talk to. . . . We tell them the truth; it's a win-win situation. You can win-win with them all day long, and they will find fault with it. One engineer told me point blank that he would not pick up the phone and report anybody. I said, "We're not asking you to report anybody. What we're doing is getting them off the property; they can come back to work the next day." He said, "Well, I'm still not going to do it; I feel like I would be reporting them." I said, "Now you've got an alternative. Tell me which is better: to pick up the phone and mark me off RedBlock or go out with me and get caught. I'll go to the EAP counselor and be back in thirty, sixty, ninety days, if I don't get fired for a Rule G. And you'll go home fired forever under Rule E [which requires co-workers to report their co-workers' alcohol and other drug use to management].

Nonetheless, many railroaders continue to think of Operation:Red-Block as a "snitch" program. One brakeman, whose life and job had been saved by the program, told us that he still had difficulty getting co-workers into Operation:RedBlock because he had "trouble ratting on anybody about anything."

Workers who are concerned about losing their jobs also delay getting help. For instance, a worker who had used the program's mark-off provision because he had been drinking at a New Year's party delayed seeking treatment for his cocaine addiction because he feared losing his job. When management caught him in a random drug screen, he became frantic. He was still concerned that his job was at risk when his union became involved:

> I didn't know whether I had a job. . . . The head of the Operation:RedBlock committee is also my union man. And all he told me was, "Don't worry about it. You're going to have your job. It's being turned over to Operation:RedBlock. But the company doesn't hold this against you. You're now in somebody else's hands." That was kind of reassuring but I had family and bills. . . . I still didn't know what to expect because there weren't set steps. . . . That's why I'm involved in Operation:RedBlock [as a committee person] . . . to make sure there are some guidelines . . . to reassure the employee that this is for you. That you are going to have a job.

Some teams have even begun to develop their own substance abuse referral networks in order to further distance themselves from the company EAP and assure workers that they will be protected from harm if they seek help.

Proposition 3.5: Although they remain committed to a nondisciplinary philosophy, successful MAPs still use job performance as a criterion to identify union members with problems.

Ideally, MAPs attract union members before they become entangled in the disciplinary process. Unfortunately, many workers do not voluntarily seek help for personal problems either because they deny having the problems or because they believe they can manage the problems themselves. Likewise, co-workers may be uncomfortable giving workers who have personal problems unsolicited advice. Job performance provides a legitimate rationale for intervening and encouraging one's co-workers to seek help from the MAP, as one coordinator commented:

> You don't confront people with the fact they have a drinking problem. The concept we took away [from our MAP training] was that you confront them with, "You may not have [an alcohol] problem, but when you are on the property under the influence, you are a [performance] problem and, if you have a drinking problem, then there is help available to you.

At both CSXT and Amtrak, a procedure for maintaining job performance standards is built into their Operation:RedBlock programs. For example, when an individual reports to work under the influence of, or in possession of, alcohol, a co-worker can simply mark the individual off, which automatically protects him from being charged with a Rule G violation and discharged. When the worker is safely off the property, members of the terminal's Operation:RedBlock team talk with him to determine whether he needs assistance for an alcohol or drug-related problem.

Members of the AFA's EAP invoke the job performance standard more subtly, but the function is the same: to signal that something is wrong and justify a peer counselor's intervention. For example, one AFA EAP peer counselor told us how she learned about a bulimic flight attendant:

> I got a call from some crew members about her. I called her and said, "We are getting reports that you are eating half the crew meals and going into the bathroom and throwing up. Your color is also bad. We know that you've had a problem in the past. You need to see a doctor. . . . She thanked me for my concern.

The flight attendant did not immediately accept help from the peer counselor; however, the intervention made her aware of the union's concern. Subsequently, when her performance deteriorated further and her supervisor threatened disciplinary action, she requested help from the AFA peer counselor to "get [the supervisor] off her back."

Proposition 3.6: MAPs are more successful in achieving their potential when locally based peers serve as the counselors.

In the 1960s and early 1970s, most management-based EAPs were on-site programs staffed by professional social workers or recovering alcoholics employed by the company. Although the staffs of the local EAP offices often reported to some central, corporate EAP administration, they usually were autonomous and relied more on their relations with employees in the local facility and surrounding community than on contacts at the corporate level.

As managers became more cost-conscious, they increasingly hired external EAP contractors and later managed-care providers to take over their EAP services. These agencies claim to offer services similar to those the on-site EAP staff provided but at lower costs because they were off-site and thus benefiting from an economy of scale. Many of the off-site services, however, especially managed-care providers, only operate toll-free phone lines staffed by counselors to whom clients explain their problems. The counselors conduct a preliminary assessment over the phone and then refer the callers to an affiliated care provider.

MAPs operate entirely differently. In all three programs we examined, the MAPs' activities centered on the teams of volunteer peer counselors at the local work units (regardless of whether these units were moving or stationary). By focusing on the local level and by providing local teams with a high degree of autonomy, all three programs maximize their access to unit- and occupation-based subcultures and peer networks. It is the access to these subcultures and social networks that is so critical in gaining the trust of union members and in ensuring that workers refer their troubled colleagues to the MAP.

All three programs have locally based committees and teams, but in some programs, the administrative structures are more centralized than in others. For example, local committee members at the AFA EAP complete a standardized client data form for each case they handle and then send the form in to the AFA's national EAP office for inclusion in a nationwide database. By contrast, team members in the CSXT and Amtrak Operation:RedBlock programs keep no records.

We found no evidence that the more formal and centralized structure of the AFA EAP made its committees less successful than those at CSXT and Amtrak. Indeed, there is some evidence that some centralized control can be useful in identifying and solving programwide problems, helping peer counselors handle the demands of managed care, and introducing beneficial new techniques and strategies, such as crisis intervention teams to handle issues related to workplace trauma. For instance, the AFA EAP, under the guidance of Dr. Barbara Feuer, has been a pioneer in the development of crisis intervention programs, and her team of peer counselors, which is made up of individuals from across the country, can be readily mobilized to help members when such traumatic incidents as plane crashes occur. In addition, by tracking national trends, the AFA EAP is also able to focus its outreach efforts by targeting groups of attendants with special problems.

Some programs had no local committees, either because members had recently resigned and not yet been replaced or because a site or work unit had only recently been integrated into the union. In these cases, the union's national MAP office was forced to provide off-site service, typically via telephone.

Centralizing the activities of an MAP, however, can also severely limit the program's effectiveness for several reasons. First, almost all the clients who call a centralized phone number are self-referrals, which means that other types of referrals may be shortchanged. In those few cases in which peers contact the national office to refer a local co-worker, the Washington-based, off-site staff must take action from hundreds, if not thousands, of miles away, which is often difficult but not impossible to do. Second, unlike local peer counselors, who are usually able to establish some rapport with local management, off-site counselors never receive referrals from supervisors. Third, and finally, follow-up activity is extremely limited. Information regarding reabsorption problems, for example, cannot be culled from the local gossip network. At best, follow-up activity is limited to an occasional phone call.

Proposition 3.7: Utilization of an MAP declines as the size of the work unit increases and increases as the size of the MAP committee increases.

The most basic problem any MAP committee faces is how to reach all parts of the occupational community. For example, although flight attendants share a common work culture (Salaman 1974; Van Maanen and Barley 1984; Sonnenstuhl and Trice 1991; Volpe 1982), there are also independent communication networks, which are only loosely tied to one another through a few individuals. To communicate its message as broadly as possible, the AFA EAP committees attempt to recruit peer counselors from each network or subculture. This strategy has a basis in social science research, which suggests that information travels from one segment of a social system to another via the weak ties that link one part to another (Granovetter 1973, 1983; Collins 1988). Applied to the use of medical services, for instance, this notion suggests that individuals will not use a new health program until someone in their communication network tells them about it (Maida 1984; Freidson 1970).

In examining the railroaders' and flight attendants' MAPs, it became obvious that their committees' ties to the many social networks in their work units became increasingly tenuous as the size of the work units increased and, consequently, as the number of social networks increased. According to the peer counselors, the solution is to increase the size of the local committee so that it can cast a wider net. By increasing the size of the local committee relative to the size of the work unit, peer counselors can gain access to many networks and eventually develop the trust individuals need to refer themselves and others to the MAP. In order to test this belief, we used the AFA EAP's computerized case data from 1990. For the seventeen local committees included in the data base, we found a positive correlation ($r = .47$ $p < .10$) between the relative size of an MAP committee—that is, the ratio of committee members to the number of employees in the work unit or facility—and the committee's utilization rate (the percentage of union members in a unit or facility who have contact with the MAP in the course of a year). These results suggest that successful MAPs will be composed of a growing number of peer counselors who link the program to all subcultures within the union.

Proposition 3.8: The greater the similarity between peer counselors and co-workers, the greater the utilization rate.

Another belief of the peer counselors is that program utilization is increased by having a committee whose composition reflects that of the groups they seek to help. Within the Operation:RedBlock programs, for instance, team members believe that, when they must confront someone such as a locomotive engineer, it is best to have an Operation:RedBlock member from the individual's craft on the team. Similarly, the peer counselors on some AFA EAP committees were concerned that their committees were composed of older, more experienced flight attendants while most of their co-workers were younger and had less seniority. They felt that access to these flight attendants could be maximized only by ensuring that the demographic makeup of the committee at each home base reflected the flight attendant population at that location. Our analysis of the AFA EAP data for 1990 suggests that this concern is well founded. We found that local committees, which were made up predominantly of less senior flight attendants, had higher utilization rates than those predominantly made up of more senior flight attendants (r = − .51, p < .10). This may occur for two reasons. First, troubled flight attendants are encouraged to voluntarily seek help from the program by the positive examples provided by committee members whom they perceive to be like themselves. Second, younger peer counselors are part of the same network as younger flight attendants and therefore able to more readily identify those who needed help and encourage them to use the program. These findings suggest that in order for MAPs to be successful, they must recruit peer counselors who reflect the union's basic demographics.

Our data from AFA EAP, however, also suggest that too much dissimilarity with regard to seniority may retard utilization. We found that as diversity with respect to tenure increased, utilization of MAPs declined (r = − .49, p < .10). Our interview data suggest that this may be because committees composed of members from the same backgrounds may be better able to work together than committees composed of members with highly dissimilar backgrounds, especially with regard to tenure. Consistent with recent organizational research (e.g., Zenger and Lawrence 1989), peer counselors may find it easier to communicate among themselves when their local committees are composed of either predominantly junior or predominantly senior employees, and this arrangement may make it easier for them to promote the program among their troubled colleagues.

Proposition 3.9: The larger the number of recovering members who are active in a union's MAP, the more successful the MAP will be in achieving its objectives, particularly those related to substance abuse.

In all three programs we examined, peer counselors consistently noted that, to reach substance abusers, workers who are in recovery must serve on the local committees. An Operation:RedBlock coordinator described the ideal mix of committee members to investigate an individual on mark-off: "The perfect confrontation committee would be an AA [member], a teetotaler, and a user who doesn't abuse. . . . That way you've got all your bases covered. . . . There is no way that guy who is addicted can say anything because that guy who is recovering can refute it."

Early job-based alcoholism programs were often started by members of Alcoholics Anonymous who enlisted the cooperation of industrial physicians in their efforts to help other suffering alcoholics (Trice and Schonbrunn 1981). Although AA members believe that only another alcoholic can help an alcoholic gain sobriety (Alcoholics Anonymous 1939; Rudy 1986; Denzin 1987), they also believe that nonalcoholics, both professional and nonprofessional, have important roles to play in the prevention and treatment of alcoholism. According to this logic, which has been adopted by other self-help groups, such as Narcotics Anonymous (Hurvitz 1974), nonalcoholics, particularly professionals, can help alcoholics by destigmatizing alcoholism and encouraging alcoholics to affiliate with the twelve-step program, but they can never truly understand what it means to be an alcoholic. This belief is evident in other union programs, especially those dominated by members of AA (Sonnenstuhl and Trice 1987), and all three programs we examined endorsed it. Consequently, the peer counselors in the AFA EAP believe that, for their program to attract chemically dependent flight attendants, their local committees should be composed of workers who can act as examples for those still suffering from alcoholism and other drug addictions.

Although most of the peer counselors we interviewed believed that including recovering alcoholics on MAP committees was essential, our analysis of the AFA EAP utilization data from 1990 provided only weak support for this notion. The proportion of local committee members in recovery was indeed positively associated with the utilization rates for problems associated with chemical dependence. The link was weak, however, and lacked statistical significance.

Two unique characteristics of the AFA EAP program may explain this finding. First, all the AFA's peer counselors, including those who are not in recovery, have been socialized to believe that having counselors who are in recovery is essential in motivating chemically dependent flight attendants to use the EAP. That the nonrecovering peer counselors convey such an attitude about recovery may be sufficient to attract workers to the program. Second, many friends and supporters of the AFA EAP are members of AA or Narcotics Anonymous; as these friends become known to chemically dependent flight attendants, they act as examples for them and encourage them both directly and indirectly to use the EAP. If these explanations are correct, the percentage of peer counselors in recovery may be less important in motivating chemically dependent co-workers to use an MAP than the program's attitude toward recovery and the examples provided by friends and supporters.

Proposition 3.10: In successful MAPs, peer counselors work closely with members of other union committees but still maintain some distance from everyday union affairs.

A common characteristic of all the MAP committees and teams we examined is that they maintained some distance from everyday union affairs. The peer counselors saw their MAP work as outside the normal realm of affairs that union officers and staff attended to and felt that it was important to avoid letting MAP issues become the subject of labor-management haggling.

Several peer counselors in the AFA EAP referred to the program as an "oasis" in what to them was a "desert" of labor-management relations. They were afraid that if the EAP became too closely identified with other aspects of union activity, they would lose their ability to work cooperatively with management on issues that could affect members' very lives.

At the same time, no MAP can operate in a vacuum. Contact with national and local union officers and agencies is not only required but is probably desirable for the sake of the program. Our data indicate that MAP committees that maintained close contact with other union committees had the highest rates of program referral and utilization and consistently achieved high rates of success in treatment (i.e., a high proportion of those referred to treatment returned to work and maintained sobriety at least throughout the first year).

Which committees should a local MAP team maintain contact with and why? In the three programs we examined, the local MAP groups maintained close contact with members of their local's grievance committee. It was not at all unusual for a grievance committee member to refer clients to the MAP. Thus, the members of the grievance committee were often able to provide a means of early MAP intervention.

Grievance committee members also referred union members to the MAP as a way to protect them from further discipline. For example, a grievance committee member might directly refer a flight attendant to the MAP, suggesting that, if the flight attendant took care of his or her problems, the union would have a better chance of winning the grievance. In such cases, the threat of supervisory discipline often gives the MAP leverage over the troubled worker, thus easing the process of convincing the worker to seek help.

In the AFA, local MAP committees either functioned as the union's professional standards committees or were in close contact with them. Regardless, MAP committees would hear about violations of accepted standards. Most of these violations were minor. Those that were more serious, however, often pointed out to the MAP committee flight attendants who were chemically dependent. Thus, like a grievance committee, a professional standards committee can provide an important early warning and access to those social networks that peer counselors have been unable to penetrate.

Sometimes, MAPs work with other union committees. For instance, many Operation:RedBlock committees work with safety committees because, as one team member said, "In the course of talking RedBlock, [we] automatically talk safety; particularly the engineers are likely to stick in a little life-saving talk." In addition, the coordinators of Operation:RedBlock have encouraged RedBlock's committees to use safety committee events to spread information about the MAP more widely:

> We have urged the RedBlock committees to take advantage of the network the company has in place through the safety committees. The safety committees have funding that ORB [Operation:RedBlock] does not have. So, by working with them, we are able to capitalize on what is happening without generating additional costs, as well as getting them to work together, which is our ultimate goal.

In the AFA, some MAP committees also work closely with the hotel committee, which is responsible for deciding with management which hotels flight attendants stay in during layovers. The MAP has been instrumental in encouraging the hotel committee to push management to reject or select certain hotels at several locations. The MAP at one local encouraged the hotel committee to work with management to identify alternatives to a rather isolated hotel known for its party atmosphere. Members of the MAP committee felt that although some flight attendants enjoyed the atmosphere, others, particularly those in recovery, would have preferred to stay in a less isolated location where there would be less risk of slipping back into drinking. Similarly, some Amtrak Operation:RedBlock committees have worked to improve housing conditions for railroaders away from home.

Proposition 3.11: The more comprehensive and continuous the peer counselors' training, the more successful the MAP will be in achieving its objectives.

Comprehensive, ongoing training is essential to program success. Training may take a variety of forms. It may be provided formally in a classroom, or it may be provided informally on the job. The critical point is that the training must be ongoing to enable the peer counselors to grow as the program evolves.

The AFA EAP's training program is designed to accommodate the changing needs of union members as well as the growing skills and interests of the peer counselors. New recruits go through a rigorous one-week basic training program with flight attendants from other domiciles and airlines designed to teach them facilitative counseling skills and to provide essential knowledge they can use in establishing a network of community services within their home domiciles. Once peer counselors learn these basic skills, they are eligible to participate in an advanced training program, which focuses on such special topics as preventing burnout and treating eating disorders. Committee members also develop their own interim training programs, tailored to the special needs of the counselors and union members in their domiciles. Beyond providing essential knowledge, the AFA EAP's training activities charge up the peer counselors and prevent burnout and workplace trauma. One committee chair told us:

> I think I could do a better job if I could get ten hours a month or something like that just doing EAP work, you know, getting some sort of compensation. I really think that would help us stop getting burned out. It's hard to put in eighty to eighty-five hours of flying and then come home and deal with these problems. I did much better when I was flying only fifty hours. I

did great. I was productive. I didn't feel burned out. I felt good about what I was doing. I felt that I made a difference. But to do this on top of a full-time work, well, I think the program is going to end up losing some really good people. . . . Every year, every two years, we're forced to get new members to replace the burned-out ones and then start all over with the training. Wouldn't it make more sense to hang on to the ones that are already here by constantly giving them more training and in the process recharging their batteries—like with me and this last advanced training?

Like the AFA's EAP, Operation:RedBlock at CSXT places a high value on training as a way to retain MAP committee members. This is especially necessary in that members of Operation:RedBlock committees, unlike the members of the railroad's safety committee, do not get paid for their committee work.

PROGRAM MAINTENANCE

It is important for an MAP to be structured so that it does not become vulnerable to shifts in labor-management conflict and cooperation. MAPs depend for their success on their ability to engender trust among union members, and as such, cannot become captive to the political whims of a union nor dependent on management for its support. To a large degree, an MAP is *of* the union, but it is also *independent* of the union. Similarly, although it may need the assistance of management, it must remain totally autonomous of management. As such, a successful MAP must hover delicately above the daily politics of labor-management relations, as one CSXT coordinator observed.

This whole process hinges on one word: *trust!* To get people empowered with the ability to effect change, they have to be able to trust that the people responsible for our railroad are going to support them, are going to be receptive to their ideas, their thoughts, their philosophies. . . . They are building trust daily within those committees and the activities they do. They're starting to trust. . . . Trust has to be there, and that's something you earn. It has to be earned on labor's side, and it has to be earned on management's side. We're there, not 100 percent, but we're there. It's a matter of maintaining that trust and not letting the other side down.

Although MAPs should seek to be independent of management, they must act within the context of existing labor-management relations. Consequently, MAPs must be understood against the backdrop of the ongoing relationships between the unions and companies involved.

These relationships may be conflictive or cooperative, and they are likely to change over time.

Proposition 3.12: The less an MAP relies on management for the day-to-day financing of program operations, the more successful it will be in balancing the dual goals of autonomy from and cooperation with management.

Within the context of current labor-management relations, unionists often feel it is desirable for management to pay union members to participate in some activities that are in management's interest. This sentiment can be traced to the principles of industrial unionism guiding labor-management relations. According to these principles, management is responsible for organizing work and, in return for fair wages, labor is responsible for carrying out management's directions. Unionists argue, for example, that being a member of a safety committee is extra work for which the employee should be compensated, even though it is in the union's interest to protect its members' safety.

In contrast, members of Operation:RedBlock committees attribute part of the program's success to the fact that they do not get paid for their work on RedBlock:

> The only truly volunteer program is Operation:RedBlock, and that is what made it fly. That's what gave the people the ability to sell it or give it away to their peers. We're not doing this because the company is paying us. We're doing this because we care about our workplace; we care about our brothers and sisters. We have a right to effect change. . . . It gives [members] a sense of ownership and a greater sense of pride in what they are doing. . . . [Our] response to management is, "We don't want your money. We want to own it [RedBlock]. We want to run it. You trust us to take care of the problem, and we'll trust you to support us when we need your help in a mark-off situation." There's the big difference.

In addition, unlike an EAP, Operation:RedBlock is a union-owned program. Remarks by one RedBlock team captain typify this widespread sentiment:

> RedBlock is supported by CSXT, and the support we get is that RedBlock has the final say. We have a right to say, "Yes, this man has finished treatment. Yes, this man is going to his aftercare program. And, yes, this man is going back to work." We don't have that fear of someone slamming down the gavel and saying, "No, he's not!" We have to keep the upper hand in that situation.

All three programs differ in the sources of their financial support. The AFA EAP is financially independent of the airlines, and the Operation:RedBlock programs, although they remain dependent on management to underwrite their costs, have explored alternative mechanisms for making themselves more financially independent. In each case, however, one critical element that fosters some of the financial independence is the spirit of communal voluntarism. For instance, all the programs have recently had their operating budgets cut, forcing them to scale back training for peer counselors. Given the importance of continuous and comprehensive training, the coordinators are worried about the future. At CSXT, the coordinators fear that the cutbacks may seriously impair the program, and one commented:

> We've done a pretty good job of training folks in the first two rounds of training, but there are a lot of new people coming into the system who need training. Also, we need to reinforce what we've told people. We've also learned some new things which need to get into the system. . . . It's true we've got these RedBlock members all fired up, but we've got to keep them fired up with the training. It's all well and good to say people are willing to volunteer their time, money, and energy, but you need to give them a little something back to keep them going.

Ultimately, however, the program directors believe that the MAPs will survive because of their members' commitment to the principles of voluntarism and mutual aid. One coordinator for CSXT put it this way:

> The members are going to continue this program with or without us because they have seen the benefit of what it has done. The people are so involved [in helping one another] that we're not going to change. We've changed the culture. . . . Institutionalization comes from doing it so long that it changes the culture. . . . You change the culture by changing one mind at a time; one attitude at a time. . . . In Cincinnati, one person stood out, . . . the local chair who was so adamantly opposed to this program that he would fight you. I left there with him as a supporter. One person at a time. . . . The members have seen what this program has done, and they're not going back to the old days.

Proposition 3.13: The more positive the quality of labor-management relations, especially between supervisors and workers, the more successful the MAP will be in achieving its objectives.

As the program coordinator suggested, the success of the CSXT's MAP partially hinges on the trust established between management and labor, or between supervisors and peer counselors. This relationship was aptly described by the director of CSXT's Operation:RedBlock program:

> When you get beyond the executive level, there isn't anyone out there, whether they are a manager or a labor representative, who doesn't know exactly how this thing [the MAP] works. [If] you get out of the general chairman's office, everybody knows how it works because they use it. They depend upon it working. It's a solution that works, and they are going to continue to use it.

In contrast, one coordinator credited Amtrak's chief operating officer with setting the tone for labor-management cooperation in each of its divisions:

> If it wasn't for our chief operating officer we wouldn't be here today. Other managers saw his commitment to RedBlock; as a result, it gave us a chance to explain to them. He attended every division implementation and was fluent in the procedures.

Labor-management trust is especially crucial between supervisors and peer counselors because supervisors retain the right to discipline workers, and the counselors remain responsible for protecting the rights of union members. Cooperation between both parties is often essential for saving workers' lives. When cooperation is lacking, supervisors may end up simply disciplining troubled workers rather than offering them an opportunity to solve their problems. One AFA peer counselor underscored the value of having a cooperative labor-management relationship:

> I usually liked to start out by saying "I'm your EAP. I understand you're having some problems. I'd like to help you. I'd like to talk." If the [flight attendant] swung automatically right into the denial phase, I would have to say, "Well, I have to tell you your supervisor told me that I need to call you. And I think it's in your best interest at this point that you get honest with me and tell me what's going on."

How willing supervisors are to use their muscle to motivate workers to accept help is clearly an important determinant of an MAP's success.

Data on the AFA's EAP confirm that having a positive labor-management relationship is also important in identifying substance abusers. In our analysis of AFA's 1990 data, we found a significant relationship between the quality of labor-management relations and the percentage of total cases categorized as chemically dependent (r = .58, p

< .05). As the quality of labor-management relations improved, supervisors became more likely to work with the AFA EAP peer counselors to ensure that chemically dependent flight attendants received help. We also found that the quality of labor-management relations is related to several characteristics of the local MAP committee. Younger peer counselors who are relatively new to a unit were more likely than older counselors with seniority to develop cooperative relationships with local supervisors. These findings complement Trice and Beyer's earlier findings that younger, lower-ranking union officials are more likely than older, higher-ranking officials to develop cooperative relationships with management concerning the handling of alcoholics (1982).

Ultimately, labor-management relations must be characterized by trust, and both sides must be willing to nurture the relationship if the MAP is to reach its full potential. A CSXT coordinator summarized this finding:

> No other company in the railroad industry has what we've got, and they won't have it as long as they are structured [top-down] the way they are. I don't see why this type of program, this type of caring, this type of trust couldn't be put into any industry or any business in this country, as long as management is willing to work [with labor].

Proposition 3.14: The more positive the quality of the MAP's working relationship with its employer's internal and external health care referral agents and providers, the more successful the MAP will be.

Although an MAP is union-based, it cannot operate independently of the company's EAP, where one exists, or the company's insurance provider. Where a company EAP exists, labor must develop a working relationship with its counselors. As we saw at CSXT and Amtrak, staff of the company's EAPs refer substance abusers to treatment. It is therefore critical that the members of the MAP committees feel they can trust the counselors in the management-sponsored program. One coordinator reported,

> We tested [the EAP counselors] by giving them information that they had the opportunity to pass on, and they didn't do it. That established a belief with us that we can trust these guys. We can depend upon them to do what they need to do. But staying within our role is one of our main objectives. EAP counselors deal with the problem. We deal with getting the problem off the railroad and identifying [a problem] early enough so that the EAP counselor can do something about it. I think that is the main key to our success.

Establishing this level of trust is difficult. As we have already mentioned, some Operation:RedBlock committees at Amtrak, for example, do not trust the counselors in their EAPs and have begun making their own referrals.

MAP counselors must also know how to work with their companies' managed-care providers. This may require knowing the providers' jargon, being an advocate for troubled members, and identifying alternative forms of care for workers.

All three MAPs we studied have had their referral efforts stymied by corporate managed-care providers. For instance, the AFA's peer counselors can no longer refer alcoholic flight attendants directly to treatment; they must first receive approval from the provider. In adapting to this requirement, the AFA's peer counselors have had to teach the providers why treatment methods appropriate for other workers may be inappropriate for flight attendants:

> [The managed-care group] feels very strongly about doing things outpatient rather than inpatient. . . . They say you can't take people out of their environment, put them in this safe environment for thirty days and then all of a sudden let them loose. They claim that it is much easier for them to learn to function if they've kept with their jobs and their everyday routine and learn as outpatients to deal with their problem. It makes a lot of sense, except when you're a flight attendant. Why? Because you don't have a nine-to-five job. That's one of the things that we have to try to teach the managed-care folks.

SUMMARY

This chapter has presented a number of recommendations to guide unions in ensuring that the spirit of communal voluntarism is a fundamental component of their MAPs and in structuring an MAP to ensure that the program will achieve its full potential. It is particularly important to have peer counselors who sincerely want to help their co-workers and to have the union leadership's support. Ideally, the union should support the MAP's overall mission of enhancing members' emotional well-being and provide financial resources to the program. Finally, it is necessary to integrate the MAP into workplace and union activities. MAP committee members must work closely with other union committees and cultivate positive working relationships with supervisors. These relationships are critical to establishing and maintaining the ethic of communal voluntarism essential to MAPs.

4

PROVIDING HELP AND REFERRAL

Communal voluntarism means peers helping peers. In an MAP, how-ever, helping takes on many meanings. It means motivating chemically dependent and other troubled workers to seek treatment for their problems, referring those workers to appropriate community-based agencies for treatment, and supporting those workers during their recovery. Helping also means working to prevent those problems from occurring in the first place. In this chapter, we examine how MAPs may organize the processes of helping to ensure that workers seek help for their problems and receive high-quality treatment.

Just as the three MAPs in our study vary significantly in their focus, they also vary in their methods of referral. The AFA's EAP tries to help flight attendants with a wide variety of problems. Peer counselors refer troubled co-workers and family members to helping agencies within the community, and they follow up after treatment. In contrast, the em-phasis of the CSXT and Amtrak Operation:RedBlock programs is preventing substance abuse. Members of Operation:RedBlock teams refer co-workers in need of treatment to the company's EAP, where professionals assess their problems and refer them to treatment agen-cies within the community. Sometimes, team members refer co-workers directly to treatment agencies.

MOTIVATING WORKERS TO SEEK HELP

Help-seeking is an interactive process in which troubled workers seek and receive advice about their problems from other workers (Son-nenstuhl 1990). Some workers ask for help directly, either from their co-workers or from the union's peer counselors; other workers may be unaware of their problems or actively deny they have any.

Peer counselors play both proactive and reactive roles. In their proactive role, they provide their co-workers with unsolicited advice and support. In their reactive role, they provide solicited advice and support. Several guiding propositions follow from the basic notion that help-seeking is an interactive process.

Proposition 4.1: In successful MAPs, the key tools used to motivate co-workers to seek help and, in the case of substance abuse problems, to maintain long-term abstinence are trust and occupational identity.

In all three programs examined, trust is a key component of the help-seeking process. Workers generally feel more comfortable seeking and receiving help from the peer counselors than from professional counselors associated with a company program. There are two reasons for this. First, because MAPs are peer-based rather than corporate-based, workers are not afraid of being disciplined if they seek help from an MAP; they view the peer counselors as helping them to resolve their problems and ultimately as helping them to save their families and jobs. Second, the workers feel that the peer counselors understand their problems better than professionals because they are members of the same occupation.

An Operation:RedBlock team captain highlighted the importance of trust in convincing workers to seek help from an MAP and particularly in assuring them that they will not be disciplined for doing so:

Trust is the key element which it takes to make this program work. . . . When [employees] were able to see how the thing worked, they developed trust in it. They saw that their brothers and sisters went through this thing and were able to go back to work. If they went to treatment, they came back and were the salesmen saying, "Yeah, this thing really did save me, really did help me, really helped my family." This convinced the other employees that this really is an employee program.

Another Operation:RedBlock team captain emphasizes the importance of occupational identity in motivating employees to seek help, particularly when they are suffering from substance abuse problems:

With the inception of RedBlock, we found that no one could help a person except his own [union] brother. The peer pressure of alcoholism is when you drink with your brother; in order to get sober, you have to walk with your brother as well. . . . It's the security that an employee can give his fellow worker by being there when he needs him. Being able to have a voice if an employee gets in trouble. That's the biggest thing. It's the paranoia of the railroad person, always living in fear of all the rules and government regulations. When a fellow employee or a local chairman goes in and says, "Let's do it like this!" it means a lot to him. It carries a lot of weight with that employee, and after a period of time, he begins to learn too. . . . It's not a soul-saving mission; it's a lifesaving mission. And, when you save a life, you save everything that pertains to it.

Employees also mentioned the importance of occupational identity in their seeking help from an MAP. One flight attendant, for instance, who had initially gone to her airline's EAP told us that she preferred the AFA's EAP because its counselors understood her situation better than the professionals the airline had hired:

> [The peer counselors] seemed different to me, in that the company EAP [had] somebody paid to [provide treatment] and the flight attendants were volunteers. The flight attendant volunteers that helped me had both been in treatment themselves and shared that with me. I was just real impressed with them. For one thing, they both had something that I wanted. There was a lot of serenity there. They were caring but they weren't pushy. They say it's a program of attraction rather than promotion. That's what I like about it.

Many railroaders told us that they finally sought help from Operation:RedBlock because they had seen their co-workers conquer their problems. As one recovering railroader put it, "I knew that if [Pete] could do it, I could as well." MAPs depend for their success on the positive examples recovering workers set for others.

Confidentiality is a key ingredient in all forms of employee assistance, and all employee assistance counselors are dedicated to protecting workers' confidentiality (Sonnenstuhl and Trice 1990). Still, many workers may feel uncomfortable seeking help from a company-run EAP because they fear that management may find out about their problems and use that information against them. This may be particularly true where a company and union have an adversarial relationship. In these instances, workers may be more comfortable seeking help from a union-sponsored MAP because they feel they can trust their peers when they cannot trust employee assistance professionals employed by the company. Consequently, it is crucial for the MAP to be seen as completely trustworthy and for its peer counselors to be perceived as maintaining workers' confidentiality at all costs. The consequences of not maintaining such an image were suggested by one AFA EAP committee chair who told us that he had difficulty gaining the trust of the flight attendants in his domicile because the previous chair of the EAP committee had developed a reputation for working too closely with management. Workers had the impression that the committee was unable to maintain confidentiality:

> The AFA EAP at this base, in past years, broke confidentiality, and now many people do not trust [the] EAP here because of that. I understand that they were gossipy-type individuals that would go on the line and discuss cases, discuss phone calls they'd taken. It has been a very hard thing to live down, as far as I'm concerned, because even as much as not quite a year ago I had people walk up to me and tell me to my face that "I would never trust you with anything. I would never call for anything, because EAP can't be trusted." It's been difficult to deal with.

All the MAP committees put high priority on the need for confidentiality. As one coordinator of an Operation:RedBlock program put it: "From the very beginning, we have said the company would have no records. And we have been very successful in keeping the records out of their hands. That's been the most important thing in the success of this program. Jeopardize that, and nobody will trust the program."

GIVING AND GETTING ADVICE

Proposition 4.2: In a successful MAP, peer counselors, not professional counselors, interact directly with the union members.

All MAPs make use of professional counselors, but their role is different from that of the peer counselors. Peer counselors interact day to day with their colleagues, providing them with solicited and unsolicited advice about their problems. In the AFA EAP, for example, peer counselors develop their own network of community agencies and refer troubled flight attendants for treatment. The counselors consult with the professionals at the MAP's national headquarters mostly when the counselors need help in managing especially difficult cases. Similarly, in Operation:RedBlock, a team is responsible for overseeing the program at each terminal. Peer counselors seek advice from the program coordinators primarily when the problems are ones the counselors cannot solve.

In both programs, the peer counselors expressed a great deal of appreciation for the support they receive from the program's professional staff. One AFA EAP peer counselor said: "I have quite a bit of contact with national. . . . I love them. I have a great deal of respect for them, and they're very helpful. If I call and need something, I'll get it the following day. Like if I need information on resources . . . materials for a training or whatever."

A member of an Operation:RedBlock team expressed similar appreciation:

> Any time of day or night that you call these guys, they are there to help you. I mean, they never get mad at you. I don't see how they have any time with their families. I hope they do, but they are committed to it. They are there to help you. If you got a problem with somebody, they'll make it a point to be there with you. That kind of commitment means something to me. . . . I also call to consult about cases. The case consultation with them [is] good. Very helpful. Different insight into it than what I had. If I'm not seeing the light somewhere, I can call and get some suggestions from them and get some help on how to deal with it. Or something that I'm afraid of.

As the following comments from a new peer counselor suggest, new counselors are more likely than seasoned volunteers to be dependent on the professionals at national headquarters for advice:

> They are my security blanket. . . . I mean you get to the point where you are dealing with a suicidal case or a manic depressive or something that is intense that we don't have serious training other than our own gut and our own experiences to deal with. It's nice to know that there are trained professionals in that office to call.

Increasingly, however, peer counselors are assuming more responsibility for the day-to-day operations of their programs. As they mature in their role, they also feel less and less dependent on the national office:

> There's not very much [contact] anymore. I mean I used to call them all the time when I was new. I used to call them all the time. [But] now it's less and less. I only call when I need something or when there's a question. When there's been a problem, they're good. They really are good.

One way to help peer counselors mature in their role is to make sure they all understand how the MAP works. At CSXT, the coordinators have introduced retraining programs for Operation:RedBlock members. As one coordinator succinctly put it, "We have learned from our mistakes from day one, and as long as we continue to learn from them, the program will continue to grow." Another coordinator described an instance of this kind of learning:

> We would get involved where both sides had gone wrong, where they botched up a mark-off, where charges had been leveled. . . . We'd go to the division manager and say, "You've got a right to do what you're doing, but rather than build up a resentment, let us do a retraining and at the end of the retraining make an announcement that the charges have been dropped because the [workers] took part in Operation:RedBlock. Explain to them where they went wrong because they didn't know. . . . Their committees tried to make them understand how RedBlock works, but they were ill equipped at the time. So let's retrain that group and get this crew you've got charged back to work." We've done that two or three times. That's one of the things we've been able to do in order to learn from our mistakes.

Peer counselors also help one another learn and mature. One team captain of RedBlock told us how he taught some new members how to do a mark-off:

> I was working at the other end of the yard. A co-worker came to work under the influence. Another employee identified him as under the influence. . . . [The employee] didn't know what to do, so they came and got me. . . . I intervened with the employee, and we were successful in getting him off the property. Then I spent some time with those two people, educating them on how they didn't need me to do the intervention and teaching them to do it themselves.

One of the strengths of an MAP, then, is that, in general, knowledgeable peers are on the front line. How available these peers are to their co-workers largely determines whether workers will seek help from the MAP.

Proposition 4.3: In successful MAPs, volunteer counselors provide troubled workers with information about their problems and possible treatment alternatives.

In each encounter between a peer counselor and a troubled co-worker, the goal is to increase the co-worker's awareness of his or her problems and potential solutions to them. For instance, when a worker marks off RedBlock, members of the local RedBlock team meet with him to discuss the circumstances surrounding the mark-off and to assess whether the worker needs help. Comments from one Operation:RedBlock member illustrate how teams use the mark-off to educate co-workers about the program:

> He was drinking, called up, and marked off RedBlock. We [the RedBlock committee] were notified. . . . We just told him that he had done the right thing by marking off RedBlock. By doing that he helped preserve his job. He preserved his safety and the safety of his family. . . . We asked him next time to be a little more responsible when he drinks: "If you think you are going to work or if you know you are going to work, don't do it."

American culture generally discourages individuals from exercising control over others' behavior. Consequently, providing co-workers with unsolicited advice can be frightening. As one RedBlock committee member's experience illustrates, however, providing co-workers with unsolicited advice can be a positive experience:

> It was terrifying because we were still experimenting with the program. . . . The first person we marked off was my best friend. . . . We didn't know who [in management] was keeping records, although we [the unions] insisted that there be no records. . . . It was nasty. My best friend called me everything but a milk cow. . . . He challenged our friendship; he challenged my right to breathe. . . . It was tough that a friend could be so abusive, but it was because he was afraid for his job. If it had happened three months before, he would have been charged with a Rule G and fired. . . . Shortly after that mark-off, he admitted that he was wrong; he admitted that he was abusive, and our friendship continues today.

Most advice-giving situations are not as cut-and-dried as the above example. Usually, the person giving the advice has no idea whether the other person has accepted or rejected it. For instance, one AFA peer counselor, who was a recovering alcoholic, related a typical example of "jumpseat counseling" of someone she had identified as having a drinking problem. As in many cases when the peer is a recovering alcoholic or addict, she told the flight attendant her own story as a way to motivate her to recognize her problem and see how the EAP could help her:

> I was a functioning alcoholic and supposedly nobody knew. . . . I was put together. My makeup was on. I had perfumed to cover up the smell. . . . Her eyes were red, and she was in the bathroom trying to fix herself up. . . . I was trying to be nonchalant without saying I work for EAP. . . . I was just trying to get a little information out of her. . . . Well, she said that she had had a few drinks. She was up 'til two or three in the morning. She had broken up with her boyfriend. A lot of people won't say drugs on the jumpseat. But a lot of people do. She wasn't going to mention that. She was doing the same old things I used to do. . . . I could relate. I used to be there. I, once again, kind of interject my story into it so they don't feel like they're talking to somebody . . . that hasn't been there. . . . I said, "God, I know

how it is. It will be all right. I used to come to work with a hangover, and, God, isn't that the worst thing?" And she was going, "Oh, yeah. I just feel awful. . . ."I was trying to relate to it. Telling her that I knew what it was like. If she ever needed to give me a call through the EAP that she could. . . . So she goes, "Really? Well, God, that's interesting." And I said, "Yeah, I was out there partying and doing the whole shot and turned my life around. I can't tell you how much better I feel. . . ."They ache, and their interest is being piqued. . . . I gave her my card, and she thanked me. She said, "If this is a problem or this problem gets any worse, I'll call you." I said, "Okay." I just make it light . . . because I don't want to push myself or my card on somebody to have them turn against me.

Although initial attempts at advice-giving may be as nonchalant as the above example, subsequent interventions are likely to be more direct, particularly if the workers are suspected of being substance abusers and deny having any problems. In these instances, peer counselors may conspire with other workers, and occasionally with supervisors, to break through the denial and motivate the workers to accept help. One case, which an AFA EAP committee member related to us, illustrates this process:

I walked into the [EAP] office, and this pilot friend of mine tells me that this girl's going to be canned today. She's going for a meeting with her supervisor. . . . I called over to the supervisor and I said, "I understand you have a meeting today with this FA [flight attendant]. . . ." She was real uncomfortable to have to deal with this. . . . So I said, "How's your schedule look for later this afternoon? Would it be possible to put her meeting off for an hour? I'd like to talk to her."

And she said, "By all means. . . . And good luck!" . . .

I knew she was coming through the hangar. . . . I stopped her and said, "It's really critical that I talk to you for a few minutes. I understand you're in a rush, but we need to talk privately."

She was just totally like, "Who are you?" No idea what was going on.

We went off in a room by ourselves and we talked for a couple of minutes. . . . First I said, "Let me tell you what EAP is. . . ." Then I said, "I'm going to be real honest with you. Whether you know you have a problem or not, you do. And that is that you are being perceived as drinking and using drugs. I don't know if you are or you aren't. We need to talk. What's happening here with the company is you're going to go over there and you're going to be terminated or be given a last-chance type of thing, where they will mandate some sort of treatment. We need to talk seriously."

And she started crying. I remember I went over and I tried to put my arm around her, "I know how it feels. I've been in that situation and you just want to die. You'd just do anything if it weren't happening."

> She said, "No, I haven't got a problem. I don't think that's what's happening."
>
> And I said, "If you don't want to deal with me, there's some friends of yours that want to talk to you too. But if you go across the street, you'll lose your job."
>
> Then, in comes the pilot and her roommate and all that. [I] had arranged this all ahead of time in like ten minutes. [I even] called the treatment center to see if there was an opening. Called the insurance company to check on insurance. It was like into action, bang, bang, bang, bang, bang. 'Cause I knew I had one shot at it. . . . They came in, and the roommate talked about when they went to Wisconsin and she disappeared. And how scared they were, and they didn't know whether to report it to the police or not. The pilot talked about things that had been said and that he had seen her in a bar. And I said that I had gotten reports of this and that. And there was no way that she could deny it. She couldn't say anything but "What do you want me to do?"
>
> I said, "Well, I've got a plan. . . ."
>
> [The pilot] got her out there and checked her in.

Although this case turned out well, the outcomes in situations involving troubled workers are never entirely certain. This is particularly true of workers who are substance abusers, because the psychodynamics of denial are ever-present obstacles to accepting help. These are well illustrated by a case related by an Operation:RedBlock team captain:

> I took two other guys with me. I told the employee that I wanted to talk to him. We met and talked about his situation. Talked about the use of drugs. He thought first off we didn't want him using drugs on the property. We told him that we didn't want any drug use. . . . Told him he had better get his act straightened out, that if he wanted to do drugs, he better plan on quitting the railroad. If he wanted to work for the railroad, he better plan on quitting drugs. We told him about using the EAP; we educated him on how long drugs stay in the system. . . . He was very defensive, [saying,] "Well, I only use occasionally. You can't tell me what to do. . . ." I said, "You're right . . . but we can refuse to work with you if we think you are under the influence. You are the one who is going to have to prove that you are not. . . ."
>
> [Then] he got busted [in the random testing]. . . . He called us and wanted to know what we could do to help him. Told him to just go see the [EAP] counselor. . . . The best and quickest way back is to do what the EAP man tells you to do. . . .
>
> "Well, I am about to lose my house, my car. . . ."
>
> I said, "Hey, man, there is a price for everything. You chose. . . . There is nothing more we can do. . . ."
>
> He was back at work [after treatment], but he got busted again. . . . I don't like to give up hope on people, but maybe this is one of those guys born to crash.

Although this case did not turn out well, peer counselors who provide employees with treatment options tailored to their particular needs are generally able to overcome the psychodynamics of denial. This leads us to our next guiding proposition.

DEVELOPING SOURCES OF TREATMENT

Proposition 4.4: The more treatment options an MAP offers, the more successful the MAP will be in achieving its objectives.

One reason companies establish EAPs is that their health-care costs are rising. Cost is also an important determinant of the number and type of treatment options EAPs offer, especially as increasing numbers of companies contract for their EAP services with managed-care providers. For instance, the peer counselors in all the programs worry that the managed-care companies are more concerned with controlling costs than with care and are subsequently denying workers the chemical dependency treatment they need. They also complain that the managed-care providers do not understand alcoholism and drug addiction. Some also complain that they provide adequate referral options for average employees but that their needs are anything but average. By this, our respondents meant that members of their occupations had special needs and that, in order to be effective, company managed-care providers had to understand those needs and provide services accordingly. For instance, because their work schedules keep them away from home so much of the time, railroaders and flight attendants recovering from alcoholism and drug addiction often need special support services, which can be provided by the peer counselors. Consequently, we found that successful MAPs do not make decisions based on "average" employees.

Investing substantial time in evaluating treatment providers and investigating options is critical. As one Operation:RedBlock team captain told us, getting a worker into a good treatment program is the most important step the MAP can take: "If he asks for help, he's having problems. The thing I found the best is to get him into a treatment center, a quality treatment center, as soon as possible—within the next two or three hours if possible."

In the AFA EAP, it is not unusual for committee chairs to have new committee members report on treatment providers and investigate treatment alternatives as part of their training. This both exposes the new counselors to the world of treatment and ensures that they will have an ever-expanding portfolio of alternative programs from which to refer troubled co-workers.

In effective MAPs, clients are matched with treatment programs exactly suited to their mix of needs. Usually, one such need is the geographical location of the provider. Especially in the transportation industry, where many workers commute to their base from homes that are hundreds of miles away, the list of treatment alternatives must be constantly updated to ensure that workers can be treated close to their families and homes.

Other needs must be met as well. For example, it is not unusual for a flight attendant with a substance abuse problem to have an eating disorder. Thus, many MAP committees try to refer these workers to centers that specialize in both problems. Other MAP committees have made special efforts to find treatment centers that service the gay population. Finally, all the committees have tried to identify providers where the staff understands their occupations.

The chair of an AFA EAP committee serving the flight attendants employed by a small, regional carrier told us that she will refer workers to a treatment center only if it meets several basic criteria:

> First off, it can't charge outrageously. You're not dealing with United or American. When an FA says to you, "I cannot afford this," it may be denial. It may not. All I can tell you is they're telling you the truth. They cannot afford it. A 20 percent copayment is still more than your average salary—I mean, I subtract off. Look at my paycheck: nine thousand dollars plus some change this year. We don't make any money. At the least, they need to offer some sort of payment plan, and even then, you see the fear in the FA's eyes—they can't even make it through the week! And some of these people with addictions have maxed out credit cards and everything else. They're speaking the truth.
>
> Second, if you think that aftercare has got to be on Tuesday and Thursday at such and such a time and that if somebody doesn't show up for that, they're not wanting to get well, that center is not for us. If you can't work around an FA's schedule, I don't want to deal with you.
>
> Third, if you say you tell our people that they cannot have an FA life-style and still get well, I don't want to deal with you. It is harder, I'll grant you, to be an FA and get well from some of these things, but it's very, very possible. . . . If you happen to get into recovery and have the extra reward of having this neat job, good for you.

SUMMARY

This chapter has examined how successful MAPs organize the helping process; that is, the ways in which peer counselors in successful MAPs actually help chemically dependent and other troubled co-workers. Specifically, we have examined the processes of help-seeking and referral. Two of our most important findings about successful MAPs are: (1) chemically dependent and other troubled workers are motivated to seek help because they trust and identify with the peer counselors; and (2) peer counselors provide chemically dependent and other troubled employees a variety of treatment options.

5
FOLLOW-UP AND REINTEGRATION INTO THE WORKPLACE

Most treatment programs try to shelter their clients from the stresses of everyday living. The return to the workplace, however, typically forces workers in recovery to face several challenging stresses head on. Studies (Sonnenstuhl 1986, 1990) suggest that many recovering employees feel that they are on probation and subject to surveillance by managers and co-workers, all of whom are interested in one thing: whether the treatment was effective. The workplace often provided both the rationale and the social context for abusing drugs or alcohol. Returning to work may mean having to face peers who, in the past, were part of the culture of abusers. Follow-up and assistance in reintegrating recovering workers into the workplace are thus key elements of any employee or member assistance program.

The purpose of follow-up is to establish contact between the recovering worker and any one of several work-based referral agents, including employee assistance professionals and peer counselors. This contact serves two main purposes. First, it lets the employee know that he or she does not have to face the challenges of recovery on his or her own. Second, it gives the referral agent information on the worker's posttreatment status and thereby alerts the agent to any signs of a relapse.

In contrast, the process of reintegrating a recovering employee into the workplace is more structural in nature. That is, it involves helping him or her become part of a supportive work-based social network.

Often a recovering alcoholic must work with people with whom he or she once drank. In this case, the referral agent might attempt to have the worker transferred to a different unit. Occasionally, the counselor will help the recovering individual redesign his or her job or work environment. This might include restructuring the work schedule to ensure that the employee can take full advantage of his or her aftercare program.

Although EAP counselors repeatedly emphasize the importance of follow-up and reintegration, few counselors are able to perform these functions because of other demands upon their time (Sonnenstuhl 1990). This is unfortunate because research studies suggest that, when work organizations provide employees with positive social support, workers are likely to experience higher rates of long-term sobriety (Sonnenstuhl and Trice 1987; Foote and Erfurt 1991; Gordon and Zrull 1991).

ROLE OF PEER COUNSELORS IN FOLLOW-UP

Our research suggests that MAPs have the potential to be highly effective at providing follow-up because they are based in peer networks. Similarly, because they rely on volunteers from the workplace, MAPs are in a unique position to help recovering employees become reintegrated into both the workplace and the organization. These observations lead us to three basic propositions.

Proposition 5.1: The more all-encompassing the role of an MAP's peer counselors, the more successful the MAP will be in achieving its objectives.

We found that the role of peer counselors in follow-up varied not only between programs but within them. Thus, peer counselors had a far more expansive role in follow-up in the AFA's EAP than in either of the Operation:RedBlock programs. The role varied, however, even within a given MAP. For instance, within Amtrak's Operation:RedBlock, the director is attempting to build follow-up into the program:

> Originally, we would use what we called a co-worker sponsor. He or she was someone who was in recovery and was willing to be there for employees when they came back to work from treatment. Eventually, one of our team captains formed a group of recovering employees called the Employees Recovery Network. They consulted with Amtrak's EAP but had no affiliation. They would conduct closed group meetings on the property and accompany employees to meetings off the property.

The AFA EAP mandates that peer counselors attempt to maintain contact with alcoholics and other substance abusers for one year after treatment. Some local committees we studied initiated and maintained intensive contact throughout treatment and for a full year afterward. Other committees were perhaps concerned about being perceived as overzealous and simply let flight attendants who were in recovery know that further help was available.

Our examination of the AFA EAP helped us understand what an expanded role in follow-up should entail. First, the peer counselor must be willing to see troubled co-workers while they are in treatment. One peer counselor described her approach:

> If I have somebody in treatment, I always make one visit. I like it if I can talk with the counselor, because if somebody's been in treatment, then you're required to follow up for a year. You know, not every day, not even every month, but quarterly. So I like to be a part of that aftercare recommendation, and I like to explain to the therapist or the counselor what it's like to be a flight attendant, what is reasonable to expect. I do that.

Second, the peer counselor's role must be proactive in nature. Instead of waiting for the troubled co-worker to call if there is a problem, peer counselors are encouraged during training to initiate contact and maintain it for at least several months following treatment. One peer counselor told us:

> Always on the alcohol cases I'll follow up. Alcohol or drug cases where I have put them in treatment, I always want to keep an eye on them and see what their aftercare requirements are with their treatment facility. . . . On other cases, I just use my judgment.

The peer network can be an excellent source of information on recovering workers. A worker's peers are a source of gossip that could indicate that he or she is close to or in the midst of a relapse. Such information can be an early warning that it is necessary to intervene again, as in the case described by one peer counselor:

> I usually don't keep in contact for much more than a year. But a flight attendant wrote a letter to the committee saying [she] smelled alcohol on the breath of someone we had gotten into treatment [a year earlier]. I flew with some friends of this person's—a friend of hers told me that she had started drinking again. . . . And I knew I was going to be flying with her the next week. So, knowing that we needed to have a little talk, after the flight we went to her room. And she said, "Yeah, well, this is what's happened. My boyfriend and I have had a problem and we were going to split up except we bought this house together and so we have to live together." [She then told me about] all the problems that have come up. But [she said] that she

had started going back to [AA] meetings and that she was going to get back on the track and everything.

I talked to her again about a week later because she called me to thank me for being concerned and talking to her. . . . But she still has a problem. I'm going to call her again and, because my release of information has lapsed, I'm going to see if she'll sign another one. And see if I can talk to her counselor and see what [the counselor] feels is best.

In our analysis of the AFA EAP, we identified two primary ways peer counselors can help workers maintain long-term abstinence and sobriety. First, they can cement a trust-based relationship with the co-workers while they are in treatment. As one peer counselor told us, such as relationship is often essential in preventing a co-worker from suffering a relapse:

[When] I have gone and visited [people] at their treatment facility, we discuss relapse, and they know that is part of the disease, and they know that that may happen. I make sure that when they get out of treatment and if they do relapse, I want them to call me and I want to work through it with them. . . . I want to be there with them for that. [Going for treatment] may be harder than it was initially because you've really screwed up; in your mind you've really screwed up. And they beat themselves up. I ask them a lot of questions, but I haven't had the experience of having people relapse.

Second, by adopting an expanded role in follow-up, peer counselors can often provide support to newly recovering co-workers who do not get it from other sources. One peer counselor told us:

I was really basically the only one she had here. . . . When she was in the treatment center I would go and visit her once a week. Talk to her almost every day for a while in the beginning. . . . Those conversations were just like conversations of two friends, someone that is supporting her. . . . She would tell me about her breakthroughs, about the things that she was discovering about herself. Mainly she talked about her progress, where she was, how she felt, where she was today. . . . She started admitting to her alcoholism. So, we mainly talked about her feelings for her family, not having self-esteem.

In contrast to the AFA EAP, CSXT is only now beginning to recognize the importance of follow-up, ten years after it started its MAP. The interest in follow-up at CSXT comes from team members and has only recently begun to flow upward to those involved in administering the program. The coordinators of Operation:RedBlock at CSXT continue to advise its peer counselors not to take a formal role in follow-up, but participants in the program are beginning to recognize the importance of taking a limited, informal role. One coordinator noted:

> We advise people on RedBlock committees, "You take care of prevention; you take care of marking this guy off; you confront him. You find out if he does have a problem, kick him into the counselor and then get out of it." Now all of our committees, once this guy comes back, will take a little special interest in that guy. . . . They'll take a little extra time to maybe not pat him on the back but to stroke him a little bit. Tell him, "We're glad you're back and what can we do for you? Are you okay? . . ." That's sort of the informal monitoring of recovery. It's done informally without anyone saying, "We're watching you."

Several peer counselors at CSXT told us that they thought extensive follow-up is critical if alcoholics are to have successful long-term outcomes. One member of an Operation:RedBlock team commented:

> One of the keys to helping a recovering employee is that the RedBlock committee is there. If the RedBlock committee was instrumental in getting him involved in treatment, then they're going to be instrumental in helping him to maintain his sobriety. . . . Because they got him there to start with, they're not going to let him come back on the property under the influence.

Another team member noted:

> It's great to do prevention; it's great to do early identification for addiction; it's great to have an EAP there to treat them. But there is another step. The next step is helping them to maintain their sobriety after they get back into the workforce. . . . A lot of times the circumstances of the job are so burdensome, so stringent, that they cause a person to find reasons to relapse. So this is just a natural process . . . to take care of that person who is returning to work.

One reason Operation:RedBlock may have been slow in developing the peer counselor's role in follow-up is that the division of labor in the program is between union-based peers and management-based professionals. In RedBlock, unionists are responsible for prevention and for helping workers get treatment from the management-based EAP. The professionals are responsible for ensuring that individuals get the help and follow-up assistance they need.

Although this sounds like a reasonable division of labor, in reality, it is often difficult to maintain. In particular, our research suggests that many peer counselors, especially those who are in recovery themselves, find it impossible to promote prevention without also helping their co-workers avoid a relapse. The result may be that MAPs that officially focus on prevention will eventually expand the peer counselor's role to include some follow-up. One program administrator noted:

> The committees themselves have done [follow-up], but it is not something that we suggested. It's just a spinoff of what they have become involved in and interested in [doing] through RedBlock. . . . I see that as an extension of RedBlock, because the people who are involved are recovering Red-Block members. EAP puts out an aftercare plan to fulfill [its] obligations to the individual. I see these small groups as a form of the RedBlock prevention effort and education effort in helping someone maintain sobriety.

Operation:RedBlock teams that were established or dominated by recovering, and in particular, AA-affiliated, workers seem to have adopted an expanded role. One recovering railroader commented about his local RedBlock team:

> They were great when I went into treatment. [Bob, the team captain,] visited me several times in the treatment center. He told me not to worry and that when I got out I'd still be able to go back to work. He also went by the house to see if my wife needed anything. That meant a lot to me. It was a big relief knowing that they were looking out for my family. And when I came back, he let me know that the RedBlock team was there to help.

Peer counselors in non-AA-dominated groups may be apprehensive about adopting too much of a proactive role in follow-up. By contrast, counselors in groups dominated by recovering workers are especially likely to accept such a role. According to the administrator quoted above,

> some territories have formalized support groups. They say, "When you come back [to work], this group of people will be here to help you through the rough times of maintaining your abstinence." Then there are groups who say, "We're here. Call us if you need us." That's part of the growth that we're talking about: where we start taking RedBlock a little beyond the workplace and start giving the support. . . . That's where the involvement of recovering people is key, because the support group after treatment has to be people who can relate, who understand the situation. . . . Like the

railroad AA[ers] who are there and . . . understand the railroad and coming out of treatment.

Now that they recognize the value of follow-up, some administrators of Operation:RedBlock are working to restructure their training to encourage new peer counselors to take a more active role in this critical stage of recovery.

ROLE OF PEER COUNSELORS IN REINTEGRATION

Besides providing one-on-one support, peer counselors can be extremely helpful to recovering workers during their reintegration into the workplace. This leads us to our next proposition:

Proposition 5.2: The more an MAP helps troubled union members reintegrate into the workplace, the more successful the program will be in achieving its objectives.

Recovering workers confront two primary challenges when they return to work. The first is that they need to define new roles for themselves in their work-based social networks. The second is that they need to restructure their jobs, their work environments, or both so that there is a low risk they will relapse and a good likelihood they will maintain long-term sobriety. Our data suggest that, unlike most EAPs, MAPs are in an excellent position to help newly recovering workers meet both challenges.

Many employees are apprehensive and lonely when they return to work after treatment. They may imagine that skeptical peers and superiors are constantly monitoring them. They may feel that old friends have lost their respect for and trust in them.

Finally, as one recovering flight attendant reported, they may feel that former drinking partners can no longer be companions.

> When I came back to work, it was very uncomfortable for a long time. . . . I just knew that everybody thought I was just this messed-up person. And it was very difficult for me to come back. And I felt like I had to prove myself for a long time. . . . I've got a very bad record as an employee. So I literally think I didn't call in sick for two or three years. I really turned myself around in that respect. Just tried to be a good employee.

Our data suggest that MAPs are highly effective at helping newly recovering workers deal with the feelings of both apprehension and loneliness. They do this by laying the groundwork for recovering workers to become part of a non-substance-abusing peer network and by making returning employees aware of supportive social networks, such as AA, at the work site or nearby. One committee chair told us that "one thing I try to do is . . . match up a newly recovering flight attendant with someone in her area who has some time in the program, so that she has got somebody in her area to talk to."

Perhaps the most important way a peer counselor can help workers reintegrate into their work-based networks is by telling them what to expect, based on his or her own experience, and how difficult the process of integration is likely to be. One recovering committee chair told us:

> First, you come back feeling like a billboard's been put somewhere around the airport and everybody knows. And really virtually no one knows. They could really care less; they have their own lives. But that never occurs to you.
>
> Second, there's the fact you're dealing with [serving] alcohol. And because it's become such a stigma in your life. . . . You can never have it ever, ever again. There's a certain amount of resentment that everyone else is having a good time and you can't. There's the fear and isolation of having to be a "slam-clicker" [i.e., one who, upon reaching the hotel, goes straight to his or her room and avoids socializing with other crew members] on the layovers, because you don't want to have to explain to anyone else why you're not having a drink. Over time you suddenly realize, you suddenly look around through different eyes. Not everybody's having a drink. Some people have a drink, and they only drink half of it, and the rest of it sits there. You just about want to go over and slap them silly and say, "What's wrong with you?" But you can't see that at first.
>
> The first thing you want to do is isolate [yourself] with your secret. You got to be real careful you don't put yourself out there with the things that you find threatening. And over a period of time the pain of isolation equals the fear of, the threat of, being around it or having to explain it. And you venture out little bit by little bit and test the waters. You find out sometimes that it's not the world that you remembered. You didn't ever see it that way. And slowly you become more comfortable and you start functioning like everyone else. Socializing, doing things, talking about yourself. It takes a while.
>
> I say to people, don't expect to feel any better for eight months. And [meanwhile] you're going to feel like hell.

Reintegration is especially difficult in occupations in which the workers are highly mobile or isolated and in which individuals either are far from sources of peer-based social control or face geographical or scheduling obstacles to maintaining an aftercare program. In these cases, it is often necessary for an MAP counselor to help the employees restructure their jobs or work environments.

Restructuring can be done on either a policy or a case-by-case basis. Thus, restructuring might involve negotiating with management to ensure that all recovering flight attendants are not forced to spend layovers in places known for their party atmosphere. Alternatively, restructuring might involve negotiating a reduced workload or schedule for posttreatment workers. One flight attendant peer counselor told us:

> I also ask the company to give [troubled flight attendants] at least a week [off] after they come out of treatment, maybe two, to have them spend that entire two weeks getting their aftercare program well established. . . . The most important thing for their recovery is finding their groups, making sure that they can get back to their treatment center for their aftercare, dealing with the issues if they've got family. . . . Having to even question moving away from their drinking buddies toward more nondrinking people. All of those issues.

In the AFA, policy-based restructuring has been difficult because of contract restrictions regarding scheduling and trip requirements. One peer counselor admitted, "You can't expect an airline to change their whole system for a few recovering flight attendants. I mean I just don't think that is realistic. I mean I wish they could come up with some sort of way to make it easy for them; that would be great."

Another chair of an AFA EAP committee told us, "It's kind of hard to have their work rescheduled or restructured so they have an easier schedule or have less exposure, because we work with alcohol, serving alcohol. We really can't restructure schedules, because the trips are assigned according to seniority."

Thus, many AFA committees are forced to take more of a case-by-case approach. In a few, unique cases, this may involve negotiating with management to make a one-time exception to a rule. As the chair of an AFA committee noted, however, there is a tendency for committees to avoid taking such action because they fear that they will be inundated with similar requests:

> Regarding what we can do about a heavy workload, we can do basically nothing. If [recovering flight attendants] need to drop a trip, maybe we can go to the company and they'll let them not fly that trip. Or they can go to the [scheduling] board where people want to trade schedules. Maybe trade down in time with somebody [who] wants to increase time. I mean there

are all kinds of ways to adjust your schedule. As a committee, while we might have the power to get the trip dropped, I don't want to encourage that because I don't want everybody coming to me thinking that I can just drop trips here, there, and everywhere. They have to pretty much work it out themselves.

In most cases, reintegration involves counseling newly recovering colleagues on how to work around these obstacles. For example, this committee chair told us, "I'm not going to baby [flight attendants who feel they need a lighter workload]. But I will tell them where they need to go, because usually at the scheduling board, you would be able to trade with a person. Or we can trade with the commuter if there is an open trip in there."

Trip schedules sometimes make it difficult, if not impossible, for flight attendants to attend AA or NA meetings. Some are told to bring AA or NA literature with them on trips. Others are told how to find out about meetings close to their layover locations.

There is also advice for attendants who are concerned about what to do if they feel they are about to slip while they're away from home. One recovering peer counselor told us:

> I did tell the last woman that I had in treatment, [who] . . . would drink beer until she passed out, . . . "When somebody orders beer, don't open it. Don't open it. Don't get that smell. I don't even drink beer, and I open a beer on the cart—there's something about the smell of beer on the air-plane that it smells so good. Darlene, don't open it, just hand it to them with a glass over the top." She just laughed.

Such tips are included in the AFA EAP manual and are discussed at training sessions, so it is not unusual for nonrecovering peer counselors to give advice to recovering attendants on how to get around the obstacles to long-term sobriety. One nonrecovering counselor told us:

> Not having the experience myself, I follow that manual pretty closely to give people suggestions about what they can do, such as if they are feeling weak, let them know that there are AA meetings all over. And on a layover, instead of getting together with a crew, if you want to go to an AA meeting, they're everywhere and how to find them in the phone book and who to call in different cities. . . . To plan your activities in advance, so that you're not stuck with nothing to do and might find yourself wanting to drink or drug. Somebody having a weak moment on the airplane, to ask for friends of Bill W. [the founder of AA] to come into the galley in the back of the airplane for some support. And that's been done before. Right on the

> airplane. Like eight or ten people will show up. So that's a real positive
> thing that they can do at a weak moment.

Another noted:

> I always went to see people in rehab around the third or fourth week, about
> the time they would be getting out. Offer my assistance, suggestions,
> "When you go back, fly with a friend, if you can. You have to trust
> someone. It's a very dangerous time and you're out there serving liquor."

Some peer counselors go as far as to adjust their own schedules so
they can fly with a recovering colleague. Although seniority restrictions
often make this difficult, several counselors we interviewed reported
having done this. One told us that

> I have gone with people who have come out of treatment. . . . I specifically
> selected those trips to fly [with them]. People have [also] asked me to fly
> with them. And when I do, . . . they talk to me, and I can talk recovery. I'm
> not in recovery myself, but I can talk recovery. And if somebody is a little
> bit fearful of being back at work, at least they have somebody that they trust
> that they can talk to.

Finally, some counselors use a combination of reintegration strategies. They give advice, negotiate policy with the company, and, on a
case-by-case basis, help workers restructure their working conditions.

> I tell them: If you have a room that has alcohol in the refrigerator, call them
> up and ask them to remove it. You do not have to explain why. You do not
> have to give your life story. Just simply call housekeeping and ask them to
> remove the alcohol. . . . I have literally traded trips to fly the first trip back
> with a recovering flight attendant. Gone with them on that trip. Held their
> hand. Literally gone with them. And I have told them that I would do that.
> And that's where I get the cooperation from the company. The company
> helps me get onto planes and stuff like that. Or other flight attendants will
> trade with me.

*Proposition 5.3: The more explicit an MAP is about what long-term abstinence
means, the more successful it will be in achieving long-term abstinence among
individuals it assists.*

Sobriety has had many meanings over time. During the early temperance movement, sobriety meant drinking alcoholic beverages such
as ale, beer, and wine in moderation and avoiding the use of hard
liquors. For prohibitionists, sobriety meant never drinking any alco-

holic beverages at all. Today, sobriety continues to have a variety of meanings. For neoprohibitionists, sobriety means drinking responsibly by following such simple rules as "Don't drink and drive" and "Don't drink and work." For those in programs such as Alcoholics Anonymous, sobriety means following the twelve steps to an abstinent life, including helping other alcoholics remain abstinent.

Labor and management have generally adopted a pragmatic definition of sobriety: drinking that does not interfere with one's work (Trice and Roman 1978; Denenberg and Denenberg 1991). Although this definition has been useful in preventing labor-management conflict over workplace drinking, it can present practical dilemmas because it does not distinguish between problem drinkers and alcoholics. Our data suggest that successful MAPs make this distinction. They promote the idea that problem drinkers can learn to drink in moderation but that alcoholics cannot control their drinking and therefore must abstain from alcohol completely.

The distinction MAPs make between problem drinkers and alcoholics stems from the different ways members of each group respond to help. Thus, workers who are warned about the adverse consequences of their drinking and subsequently drink without suffering such consequences are defined as problem drinkers. The data from the Operation:RedBlock programs indicate that the vast majority of workers on mark-off fall into this category. After RedBlock team members have given these workers information on responsible drinking, they can drink within the limits of these guidelines.

In contrast, workers who are repeatedly warned about their behavior, who continue to drink, and who still suffer adverse consequences are assumed to be unable to control their drinking and are defined as alcoholics. An Operation:RedBlock coordinator summarized how he expects peer counselors to respond to alcoholics:

First time, give the man the benefit of the doubt, just tell him not to do it again, give him some information, education about RedBlock. . . . Second time, a pretty strong insistence that he see the EAP, realizing full well we don't have a hammer over his head but an insistence that we're not going to put up with this. This is the second time. . . . You've marked off RedBlock. [Tell him that he] may not have a problem but [he's] becoming a problem for us because we had to deal with [him] a second time. Then, the third time, we simply invoke co-worker bypass and insist he go to the EAP, because if he comes out a third time, in any normal length of time, he probably has a problem. . . . That's where we get to the point of dealing with early-stage alcoholism and drug addiction as opposed to late chronic-stage alcoholism [or drug addiction].

Although it is a matter of judgment when a worker crosses the line between problem drinking and alcoholism, recognition that a boundary exists has pragmatic consequences for peer counselors. First, workers defined as alcoholic should know that the MAP expects them to be totally abstinent. Second, the distinction between problem drinking and alcoholism provides a powerful justification for this expectation: alcoholics have been given repeated opportunities to control their drinking but were unable to do so. Third, the distinction legitimates the mobilization of resources necessary to conduct extensive follow-up. Indeed, as the data suggest, the more intensive the follow-up, the more successful MAPs will be at helping alcoholic and other drug-addicted workers abstain. One Operation:RedBlock team member who was recovering put it this way:

> The program works fine with those "normal" drinkers who have to mark off occasionally . . . but what concerns me are the alcoholics. You need to know what you're doing with them, and a lot of RedBlock guys haven't been through it. Someone who has been through it knows. . . . We don't ever give up on them. . . . That's why we're in RedBlock. We stick with them until they get it.

ENDING THE RELATIONSHIP WITH A CO-WORKER

Eventually, peer counselors must slowly and carefully end their relationships with troubled co-workers. One peer counselor described her strategy for weaning a worker she had helped:

> Initially, I did go to a couple of AA meetings to get her going. That was important stuff. But this other stuff, I mean she had to take responsibility for herself. . . . We hit a point where I found that I would [have to] be more aggressive as far as getting off the phone. You just start with little excuses at first, then that doesn't work. Then [you say,] "I got to go." Little fibs. You find yourself fibbing to get off the phone. But you know you just kind of have to cut it, otherwise she will end up taking over your life instead of you being a helper for her. I just kind of weaned her off. . . . I kind of withdrew. Maybe we hit a point where I knew she was okay. This was way down the road. I knew she was doing fine. She didn't need the intense support that she did at the beginning. I just wouldn't return her calls as soon.

SUMMARY

Although EAPs have known for years that follow-up is important for maintaining long-term sobriety, most have been unable to do so because of other program demands. Because MAPs are based in a network of peer volunteers, they offer an alternative for meeting this need. The peer counselors are present in the workplace and are able to provide their recovering co-workers support along the road to sobriety. Support may come in a variety of forms. It may be an encouraging word, helpful advice about juggling work schedules and managing colleagues, sharing a moment of inspiration from AA's twelve-step program, or going to a self-help group meeting together. Most of all, support is reintegrating recovering co-workers back into the workplace and letting them know that sobriety and long-term abstinence are possible by following the MAP's recommendations.

6

PREVENTION THROUGH CULTURAL CHANGE

Within the field of substance abuse, prevention is seen as an attractive and inexpensive alternative to treatment. Workplace prevention efforts have generally focused either on teaching workers how to reduce the risk factors associated with substance abuse or on deterring substance abuse by such punitive strategies as drug testing. Rarely has the focus been on preventing substance abuse by changing the occupational cultures that support heavy drinking and drugging as the means to constructing solidarity (Ames and Janes 1992). Because drinking and drugging are primarily male rituals for constructing communal solidarity, the following remarks are most relevant to male-dominated occupations with substance abuse cultures. Our data suggest that MAPs can contribute both directly and indirectly to preventing substance abuse by changing the drinking and drugging culture of an occupation.

Workers in drinking cultures share the belief that drinking is a central part of their work lives. Specifically, drinking is a ritual for constructing labor solidarity and highlighting workers' resistance to management. A drinking culture is not defined simply by the amount of alcohol people consume; rather, the crucial norm is that members of this workplace culture are expected to participate in drinking rituals and are required to cover up their drinking when management seeks to intervene. When newcomers arrive at work, for instance, they are often told that they must not divulge episodes of drinking to management, and they find that they are required to supply alcohol to others in their group. This binds the newcomers to their group, making them dependent on the group for survival at the workplace, both physically and socially, and creating a distinct boundary between newcomers and management.

Similarly, the influx of younger workers, who are more likely than older workers to use illicit drugs, has led to the development of drug-using cultures. Unlike drinkers, however, drug users are using an illegal substance, and older workers are likely to view them as deviant. Nevertheless, the same need for cover-up prevails both on and off the job.

Railroaders provide an excellent example of the features of an occupational drinking culture. Drinking has been part of the culture of railroading for 150 years (Licht 1983), and the culture has been highly resistant to efforts by management to change it (Mannello and Seaman 1979). Within CSXT, for instance, most crew members were part of the drinking culture. One Operation:RedBlock team captain described the culture to us:

> Most of the time, people would just get what we call "high." You know, they could still do their jobs. Every so often somebody would really get what we call "down"; we'd have to put them on the engine and take care of them; the other two men would take up the slack. We had three-man crews in those days. . . . Sometimes when a fellow would get so bad and we thought we couldn't take care of him, we'd mark him off and call someone else. We just worked 'til the person got there.

Crew members were expected to cover up for one another, as the chair of a BLE local told us:

> Because of the camaraderie of the brotherhoods, there was an unwritten rule that you don't snitch on your fellow worker. In cases where you knew about somebody who was drinking or came to work that way [drunk], or asked you to get them something [alcohol], you just didn't say anything about it. You did everything you could to cover up for them. . . . You just did not snitch on anybody. . . . You just did not associate with anybody who talked with the officials, and you did not allow anybody to get into trouble regardless of what it took to cover up for them, and that not only involved drinking but other rule violations.

Management efforts to curtail the railroaders' drinking culture have been unsuccessful. One way management has tried to deter drinking is by punishing workers for violations of Rule G. These efforts have proved futile because railroaders are not closely supervised and because management enforced the rule only selectively. According to one Operation:RedBlock coordinator, Rule G was never much of a deterrent even though "everyone knew, if you got caught, you got fired." As one RedBlock team member explained: "I'd say more or less management turned their backs at times. . . . Unless somebody really complained or they really came out and saw it . . . they more or less just turned their backs because business was booming and we needed everybody we had."

These observations suggest our final proposition.

Proposition 6.1: More successful MAPs act as agents of cultural change by constantly challenging traditional occupational norms of denial, cover-up, and enabling.

Only peers have the power to change drinking and drugging cultures that have been resistant to management change, because only they can consistently enforce the norms required to transform these cultures into cultures of sobriety. Many labor leaders may be apprehensive about trying to change occupational drinking and drugging cultures because they think such changes will alienate union members and are therefore politically unwise (Trice and Beyer 1982). It is important to remember, however, that not every union member who participates in an occupation's drinking and drugging culture believes that activities such as drinking on the job or using illicit drugs are acceptable behaviors. Many members would gladly discontinue covering up their co-workers' drinking if they knew that their co-workers would be helped rather than punished. For instance, an Operation:RedBlock team captain told us of his efforts to keep crew members from drinking and his frustration:

> I let it be known right quick that I would do something if anybody came out with me on a job either drinking or having something with them. . . . I didn't know what I would do, but I knew I would do something. I did stop a train one night. A guy set up a bar on the train . . . a suitcase with a plywood top . . . glasses full of ice. He asked, "What do you want with yours?" I said, "What the hell do you mean with mine?" . . . I asked him to put the bottle up and he refused. . . . I told him, "I'll just get another brakeman!" . . . [As a result,] he threw a brand-new bottle of whiskey out the window into a brick yard.

When unions renounce the idea of cover-up, it is important that they not appear to be reneging on their commitment to protect their members. One RedBlock team captain, who was also a chair of a UTU local, told us, "At first, I thought it was a snitch program. After attending the initial session, I realized that RedBlock was an extension of what we had been doing forever, protecting our members." Similarly, a chair of a BLE local said, "I got involved in union work to help my co-workers, and this was just another way of helping more people." Another RedBlock team member described the culture's new helping ethic:

> It's just an accepted thing. When a man's having a problem, everybody just bands together and takes care of him and helps him. Gradually, we had to realize that we couldn't do that anymore. We weren't helping the man, we were hurting him, and that's what RedBlock education has got across to people. You know, you're not helping a fellow—taking care of him and helping him along in his [drinking] problem. You need to help him overcome his problem.

Our data suggest that Operation:RedBlock has succeeded in changing the railroading culture by directly challenging its norms of cover-up. Members of Operation:RedBlock teams challenge such norms every day. In educating their co-workers about the bypass agreement's mark-off provisions, team members are helping those who suffer from substance abuse lead sober lives. There is widespread agreement among members of both labor and management that, as a result of these practices, drinking cultures have been transformed into cultures of sobriety. Members of Operation:RedBlock teams, for instance, consistently told us how the culture had changed. Comments from one brakeman were fairly typical:

> You don't see [the drinking] anymore. You don't see it, period. Like every day, eighteen years ago, you would come to work and then drink. You don't see it, period. It's not there anywhere. I knew an old switchman one time that laid in the shanty for three months drunk. They put his name on the ticket and he got paid every day. They just wouldn't bother him. They just left him back there. . . . That can't happen today.

A chair of a BLE local said:

> The attitudes of workers have changed. . . . The people have seen a better life out there, not having to worry about meeting someone who might be under the influence or. . . protecting an individual and risking their own life or job to take care of that individual. Those attitudes have changed, and people aren't going back to the old ways.

Likewise, a CSXT division manager praised the success of the program:

> Use of alcohol and drugs is no longer being tolerated by working people out there. They are regulating themselves, and I see a definite decline in the use of these types of substances. . . . [My division's random drug test]

had the lowest positivity rate of any of the divisions. . . . We attribute that directly to the RedBlock program.

Operation:RedBlock was established as a prevention program and thus has changed the railroaders' drinking and drugging culture by directly challenging it. In contrast, the AFA EAP has effected cultural change indirectly. As flight attendants become sober, they become examples for their co-workers, as one AFA peer counselor noted:

> A lot of [changing the culture] is permission. You don't have to drink. I will go out with a crew and not drink. Just have a 7-Up. And I'll say I'm having a 7-Up because I don't feel like having wine. And offer them the idea that you can go out on a layover and there is a choice. . . . I'm teaching at the same time by example. I'm choosing not to drink.

Although such behavior has an impact in the long run, our data suggest that, in order for MAPs to effectively transform drinking and drugging cultures into a culture of sobriety, the program and its peer counselors must directly challenge those beliefs and provide their co-workers with an alternative vision of their occupational community.

SUMMARY

Successful MAPs deter substance abuse by continuously challenging traditional drinking and drugging cultures in which co-workers are expected to cover up for one another's drinking and drugging. By providing alternative ways to protect substance abusers' jobs, MAPs give workers permission to relinquish that norm and substitute for it a norm of helping. With the assurance that chemically dependent workers will be treated rather than disciplined, their peers can focus on helping these workers recover from the illness of substance abuse, rather than on protecting the abusers' job.

As each worker is helped along the road to recovery, an occupation's substance abuse culture is transformed into a culture of sobriety. The process of cultural change, which is essential if an MAP is to be successful, may be the highest expression of communal voluntarism, because it demonstrates that by sticking together and helping one another, the entire group benefits.

7

SUMMARY AND POLICY IMPLICATIONS

In this bulletin, we have examined the roots of member assistance programs in communal voluntarism. We have also shown how MAPs can deter substance abuse at work, motivate union members to seek help for their problems, and help recovering workers maintain long-term abstinence.

We have noted that successful MAPs deter substance abuse in several ways:

- by furthering the union's commitment to protect its members by helping workers save their lives and livelihoods;
- by providing union members explicit definitions and expectations concerning drinking on and off the job;
- by viewing referral and long-term follow-up as part of a total approach to substance abuse prevention and deterrence;
- by challenging traditional occupational or organizational cultures characterized by denial, cover-up, and enabling to transform themselves into cultures characterized by their members' sobriety;
- by acting as agents of cultural change.

Effective MAPs use several approaches to motivate troubled union members to seek help for their problems and to ensure that troubled workers receive high-quality, cost-effective treatment:

- They develop trust based on the recognition that MAP peer counselors and workers share common occupational and social identities.
- They place a high priority on maintaining confidentiality.
- They are broad-based programs helping workers with a wide range of personal problems; however, they also maintain a special sensitivity to the problems of alcohol and other drugs.

- They provide workers who seek help information about their problems and offer them a variety of treatment alternatives.
- They refer workers to the most appropriate services available for treating their particular problems.
- They encourage workers to manage their problems over the long term by using such self-help groups as Alcoholics Anonymous, Narcotics Anonymous, Emotions Anonymous, and Overeaters Anonymous.
- They monitor the effectiveness of treatment options and regularly expand the list of treatment programs available to workers.

We also noted that effective MAPs use a variety of strategies to help recovering union members maintain long-term abstinence:

- Peer counselors maintain contact with recovering workers while they are in treatment and do not end the relationship for at least several months and often up to a year after they have completed a treatment program.
- Peer counselors take a strong role in follow-up. Especially in the cases of substance abusers, they are proactive and provide support that is both personal and emotional as well as technical and employment-related.
- Peer counselors help recovering workers adjust to going back to work. If necessary, they help them redesign their jobs and overall work environment to ease their reintegration into the workplace.
- Peer counselors do not drop their clients abruptly. Rather, they slowly wean them out of the relationship.

Finally, we must underscore that effective MAPs are able to help members because they are well implemented. If our findings highlight anything about MAPs, it is the necessity for ongoing training and education about the MAP to ensure its success. Ongoing training is necessary to ensure that peer counselors are able to perform their multiple roles and to prevent them from burning out. Similarly ongoing education is necessary to ensure that all workers are knowledgeable about the MAP and are comfortable using it. Without such training and education, an MAP will be unlikely to demonstrate successful outcomes.

The findings in this bulletin also provide the basis for several policy-related goals. First, government, management, and labor should encourage the establishment of MAPs as a means by which to make the marketplace for health care services more competitive. Making health care services more competitive would benefit all three parties because it would help ensure that more cost-effective, higher-quality services were provided. There are several ways in which MAPs could help further this goal:

- They provide clients with a broad base of information about the quality and cost-effectiveness of the services offered.
- They have accountability with clients, unlike third-party agents such as insurance companies and managed-care providers.
- Because they empower clients, former clients become an important source of referrals.

Second, federal and state governments should encourage the establishment and diffusion of MAPs. Because MAPs offer an integrated, peer-based, nonhierarchical solution to helping workers with substance abuse and mental health problems, they should interest all parties involved: labor, management, and government. Further, they are cost-effective because they eliminate the need for a staff hierarchy, including professionals and semiprofessionals, and they can provide services focused on prevention and follow-up without additional staff.

Third, government, management, and labor should look for new ways to invigorate the role of nonprofessional volunteers in helping not only workers suffering from substance abuse and mental health problems but also those with physical problems such as cancer and AIDS. The results of our study suggest that MAPs are a nonbureaucratic way to personalize employee health care. They can be an effective supplement to the highly bureaucratized prevention, referral, and follow-up infrastructure.

Fourth, government, management, and labor must begin to redefine the nature of deterrence and prevention in the workplace. They must begin to recognize that cost-effective, long-term deterrence and prevention involves changing both organizational and occupational cultures. As such, they must take steps to help workers redefine what is and is not acceptable workplace behavior, which is the key to effecting long-term cultural change. They must also recognize that, because prevention, referral, and follow-up further a greater goal, peers must play a central role in these functions as well.

Fifth, state governments should encourage education programs for MAP volunteers. Such education, however, should not be carried out by the state; rather, it should be done by nonprofit, private-sector groups such as the Labor Assistance Professionals (LAP), which is committed to offering quality education to unions and union members interested in developing MAPs. Such programs would ensure that peer counselors receive at least a minimal degree of training. At the same time, government agencies must be careful not to overemphasize credentialing

MAPs. To do so would endanger the spirit of communal voluntarism underlying the programs and discourage workers' commitment to helping one another.

Sixth, unions should reemphasize the importance of mutual aid in fulfilling their mission. They need to view MAPs as essential to their role as advocates for labor.

Seventh, management should support the initiation and implementation of MAPs. As noted above, it is in management's interest to recognize that MAPs offer a cost-effective way to deal with substance abuse and other mental health problems in the workplace. Furthermore, cooperation with labor in the area of employee health could provide the impetus for labor-management cooperation on unrelated issues, such as safety and quality.

There is still much more research to be done. We need to learn, for instance, how to prevent burnout and turnover among peer counselors and how to enhance the effectiveness of the intervention techniques peer counselors use. We hope this book has provided the basic groundwork for further examination of these and other important questions.

REFERENCES

Abbott, Andrew. 1988. *The System of Professions: An Essay on the Division of Expert Labor*. Chicago: University of Chicago Press.

Alcoholics Anonymous. 1979. *Alcoholics Anonymous: A Brief History of AA*. New York: A.A. World Services.

American Medical Association. 1993. *Factors Contributing to the Health Care Cost Problem*. Chicago: American Medical Association.

Ames, Genevieve. 1989. Alcohol-Related Movements and Their Effects on Drinking Policies in the American Workplace: An Historical Review. *Journal of Drug Issues* 19(4):489–510.

Ames, Genevieve, and Craig Janes. 1992. A Cultural Approach to Conceptualizing Alcohol and the Workplace. *Alcohol Health and Research World* 16:112–19.

Argyris, Chris, Robert Putnam, and Diana McLain. 1985. *Action Science*. San Francisco: Jossey-Bass.

Bayer, Ronald, and Gerald M. Oppenheimer, eds. 1993. *Confronting Drug Policy: Illicit Drugs in a Free Society*. New York: Cambridge University Press.

Beauchamp, Dan E. 1980. *Beyond Alcoholism: Alcohol and Public Health Policy*. Philadelphia: Temple University Press.

Bellah, Robert, et al. 1991. *The Good Society*. New York: Knopf.

Ben-Yehuda, Nacham. 1990. *The Politics and Morality of Deviance: Moral Panics, Drug Abuse, Deviant Science, and Reversed Stigmatization*. Albany: State University of New York Press.

Beyer, Janice M., and Harrison M. Trice. 1978. *Implementing Change: Alcoholism Policies in Work Organizations*. New York: Free Press.

Blocker, Jack S., Jr. 1989. *American Temperance Movements: Cycles of Reform*. Boston: Twayne.

Blumberg, Leonard U. 1991. *Beware the First Drink: The Washington Temperance Movement and Alcoholics Anonymous*. Seattle: Glenn Abbey Press.

Braithwaite, John. 1989. *Crime, Shame and Reintegration*. New York: Cambridge University Press.

Cahalan, Don. 1991. *An Ounce of Prevention: Strategies for Solving Tobacco, Alcohol, and Drug Problems*. San Francisco: Jossey-Bass.

Clawson, Mary Ann. 1989. *Constructing Brotherhood: Class, Gender and Fraternalism.* Princeton: Princeton University Press.

Cohen, Anthony P. 1981. *The Symbolic Construction of Community.* London: Tavistock Publication.

Cohen, Stanley. 1972. *Folk Devils and Moral Panics: The Creation of the Mods and Rockers.* New York: St. Martin's Press.

Collins, Randall. 1988. *Theoretical Sociology.* New York: Harcourt Brace Jovanovich.

Cosper, Ronald. 1979. Drinking as Conformity: A Critique of Sociological Literature and Occupational Differences in Drinking. *Journal of Studies on Alcohol* 40:868–91.

de Bernardo, Mark A. 1988. *Drug Abuse in the Workplace: An Employer's Guide for Prevention.* 2d ed. Washington, D.C.: U.S. Chamber of Commerce.

Denenberg, Tia S., and Richard V. Denenberg. 1991. *Alcohol and Other Drugs: Issues in Arbitration.* Washington, D.C.: Bureau of National Affairs.

Denzin, Norman K. 1986. *The Research Act: A Theoretical Introduction to Sociological Methods.* Englewood Cliffs, N.J.: Prentice Hall.

———. 1987. *The Alcoholic Self.* Newbury Park, Calif.: Sage.

Eichler, Stephen, Clifford M. Goldberg, Louise E. Kier, and John P. Allen. 1988. *Operation:RedBlock,* Rockville, Md.: U.S. Dept. of Transportation.

Eisenhardt, Kathleen M. 1989. Building Theories from Case Study Research. *Academy of Management Review* 14(4):532–50.

Erfurt, Jack C. 1990. EAP and Wellness Follow-up as Primary, Secondary, and Tertiary Prevention Strategies in the Workplace. In *Alcohol Problem Intervention in the Workplace: Employee Assistance Programs and Strategic Alternatives,* edited by P. M. Roman. Westport, Conn.: Quorum Books.

Erikson, Kai. 1976. *Everything in Its Path: Destruction of Community in the Buffalo Creek Flood.* New York: Simon and Schuster.

Etzioni, Amitai. 1961. *A Comparative Analysis of Complex Organization: On Power, Involvement, and Their Correlates.* New York: Free Press of Glencoe.

———. 1991. *A Responsive Society.* San Francisco: Jossey-Bass.

Ferguson, Charles A., and J. E. Fersing. 1965. *The Legacy of Neglect: An Appraisal of the Implications of Emotional Disturbances in the Business Environment.* Fort Worth: Industrial Mental Health Associates.

Foote, Andrea, and John C. Erfurt. 1991. Effects of EAP Follow-Up on Prevention of Relapse among Substance Abuse Clients. *Journal of Studies on Alcohol* 52 (3):241–48.

Freidson, Eliot. 1970. *Profession of Medicine.* New York: Dodd and Mead.

Glaser, Barney, and Anselm Strauss. 1967. *The Discovery of Grounded Theory: Strategies for Qualitative Research.* Chicago: Aldine.

Goode, Erich. 1989. *Drugs in American Society.* 3d ed. New York: Knopf.

Gordon, Andrew J., and Mark Zrull. 1991. Social Networks and Recovery: One Year after Inpatient Treatment. *Journal of Substance Abuse Treatment* 8:143–52.

Granovetter, Mark. 1973. The Strength of Weak Ties. *American Journal of Sociology* 76:1360–80.

———. 1983. The Strength of Weak Ties: A Network Theory Revisited. *Sociological Theory* 1:201–33.

Gusfield, Joseph. 1963. *Symbolic Crusade: Status Politics and the American Temperance Movement.* Urbana: University of Illinois Press.

———. 1975. *Community: A Critical Response.* New York: Harper and Row.

———. 1981. *The Culture of Public Problems: Drinking, Driving and the Symbolic Order.* Chicago: University of Chicago Press.

———. 1987. Passage to Play: Rituals of Drinking Time in American Society. In *Constructive Drinking: Perspectives on Drink from Anthropology,* edited by M. Douglas. New York: Cambridge University Press.

Hewitt, John P. 1989. *Dilemmas of the American Self.* Philadelphia: Temple University Press.

Hilton, Michael E., and W. B. Clark. 1987. Changes in American Drinking Patterns and Problems, 1967–1984. *Journal of Studies on Alcohol* 48:515–22.

Hitchcock, L. C., and M. S. Sanders. 1976. *A Survey of Drug and Alcohol Abuse Counseling in the Railroad Industry.* Washington, D.C.: U.S. Department of the Navy.

Horwitz, Allan V. 1990. *The Logic of Social Control.* New York: Plenum Press.

Huber, Gunter. 1991. *Computer-Assisted Analysis of Qualitative Data.* Schwangau, Germany: Ingeborg Huber Publishers.

Hurvitz, Nathan. 1974. Peer Self-Help Psychotherapy Groups. In *The Sociology of Psychotherapy,* edited by Paul M. Roman and Harrison M. Trice. New York: Jason Aroson.

Johnson, Paul E. 1978. *A Shopkeeper's Millennium: Society and Revivals in Rochester, New York, 1815–1837.* New York: Hill and Wang.

Kennedy, Valerie, and William J. Sonnenstuhl. 1992. Beyond EAPs: Peer Prevention and Intervention in the Railroad Industry. Paper presented at the APA/NIOSH Annual Conference. Washington, D.C., November 2, 1992.

Kyvig, David E. 1979. *Repealing National Prohibition.* Chicago: University of Chicago Press.

Lasch, Christopher. 1978. *The Culture of Narcissism: American Life in an Age of Diminishing Expectations.* New York: Basic Books.

Lender, Mark E., and James K. Martin. 1987. *Drinking in America: A History.* New York: Free Press.

Levine, H. G., and Craig Reinarman. 1993. From Prohibition to Regulation: Lessons from Alcohol Policy for Drug Policy. In *Confronting Drug Policy: Illicit Drugs in a Free Society,* edited by R. Bayer and G. M. Oppenheimer. New York: Cambridge University Press.

Lewis, Jay. 1985. The Federal Role in Alcoholism Research, Treatment, and Prevention. In *Alcohol, Science and Society Revisited,* edited by Edith L.

Gomberg, Helene R. White, and John A. Carpenter. Ann Arbor: University of Michigan Press.

———. 1990. CDC Reports Alcohol-Related Deaths Top 105,000. *Alcoholism and Drug Abuse Week* 2(13):7–8.

Licht, Walter. 1983. *Working for the Railroad: The Organization of Work in the Nineteenth Century.* Princeton: Princeton University Press.

Lidz, Charles W., and Andrew L. Walker. 1980. *Heroin, Deviance, and Morality.* Beverly Hills, Calif.: Sage.

Maida, Carl A. 1984. Social-Network Considerations in the Alcohol Field. In *Recent Developments in Alcoholism.* Vol. 2, edited by Marc Galanter. New York: Plenum Press.

Mannello, Timothy A., and F. James Seaman. 1979. *Prevalence, Costs, and Handling of Drinking Problems on Seven Railroads.* Final report. Washington, D.C.: University Research Corp.

Mars, Gerald. 1987. Longshore Drinking, Economic Security, and Union Politics in New Foundland. In *Constructive Drinking: Perspectives on Drink from Anthropology,* edited by M. Douglas. New York: Cambridge University Press.

McCabe, Jack 1992. Getting the Word Out. *EAPA Exchange* (January):12.

McKay, John. 1993. Boston LAP Program Promotes Expansion. *EAPA Exchange* (July):10.

Molloy, Daniel J. 1989. Peer Intervention: An Exploratory Study. *Journal of Drug Issues* 19(3):319–36.

National Institute of Medicine. 1990. *Broadening the Base of Treatment for Alcohol Problems.* Washington, D.C.: National Academy of Sciences.

National Institute on Alcohol Abuse and Alcoholism. 1990. *Seventh Special Report to the U.S. Congress on Alcohol and Health.* Rockville, Md.:U.S. Department of Health and Human Services.

Parsons, Talcott. 1951. *The Social System.* New York: Free Press.

Perlis, L. 1980. Labor and Employee Assistance Programs. In *Mental Wellness Programs for Employees,* edited by Richard Egdahl and D. C. Walsh. New York: Springer-Verlag.

Perlow, Austin. 1979. *What Have You Done for Me Lately?* New York: Routledge.

Pitts, Jessie R. 1961. Social Control: The Concept. In *International Encyclopedia of the Social Sciences,* edited by David L. Sills. New York: Macmillan.

Reinarman, Craig, and Harry Gene Levine. 1989. The Crack Attack: Politics and Media in America's Latest Drug Scare. In *Images of Issues: Typifying Contemporary Social Problems,* edited by Joel Best. Chicago: Aldine de Gruyter.

Rice, D. P., S. Kelman, L. S. Miller, and S. Dunmeyer. 1990. *The Economic Costs of Alcohol and Drug Abuse and Mental Health: 1985.* DHHS Publication No. (ADM)90-1964. University of California, San Francisco: Institute for Health and Aging.

Riemer, Jeffrey W. 1979. *Hard Hats: The Work World of Construction Workers.* Beverly Hills, Calif.: Sage.

Roman, Paul M. 1981. From Employee Alcoholism to Employee Assistance. *Journal of Studies on Alcohol* 42:244–72.

———. 1988. Growth and Transformation in Workplace Alcoholism Programming. In *Recent Developments in Alcoholism*. Vol. 6, edited by M. Galanter. New York: Plenum Press.

Rorabaugh, W. J. 1979. *The Alcoholic Republic: An American Tradition*. New York: Oxford University Press.

Rudy, David R. 1986. *Becoming Alcoholic: Alcoholics Anonymous and the Reality of Alcoholism*. Carbondale: Southern Illinois University Press.

Rumbarger, John J. 1989. *Profits, Power, and Prohibition: Alcohol Reform and the Industrializing of America, 1800–1930*. Albany: State University of New York Press.

Salaman, Graeme. 1974. *Community and Occupation: An Exploration of Work/Leisure Relationships*. London: Cambridge University Press.

Shoemaker, Pamela J., ed. 1989. *Communication Campaigns about Drugs: Government, Media, and the Public*. Hillsdale, N.J.: Lawrence Erlbaum Associates.

Sonnenstuhl, William J. 1986. *Inside an Emotional Health Program*. Ithaca, N.Y.: ILR Press.

———. 1990. Help-Seeking and the Helping Processes within the Workplace. In *Alcohol Problem Intervention in the Workplace*, edited by P. M. Roman. Westport, Conn.: Quorum Books.

———. 1994. "Sandhogs and Drinking Rituals." Typescript.

Sonnenstuhl, William J., and Harrison M. Trice. 1987. The Social Construction of Alcohol Problems in a Union's Peer Counseling Program. *Journal of Drug Issues* 17:223–54.

———. 1990. *Strategies for Employee Assistance Programs: The Crucial Balance*. Ithaca, N.Y.: ILR Press.

———. 1991. Organizations and Types of Occupational Communities. In *Research in the Sociology of Organizations*. Vol. 9, edited by Samuel B. Bacharach, Greenwich, Conn.: JAI Press. 295–318.

Staudenmeier, William J., Jr. 1985. Alcohol and the Workplace: A Study of Social Policy in a Changing America. Ph.D. diss., Washington University.

Steele, Paul D. 1989. A History of Job-Based Alcoholism Programs: 1955–1972. *Journal of Drug Issues* 19:511–32.

Strauss, Anselm. 1987. *Qualitative Analysis for Social Scientists*. New York: Cambridge University Press.

Trice, Harrison M., and Janice M. Beyer. 1982. A Study of Union-Management Cooperation in a Long-Standing Alcoholism Program. *Contemporary Drug Problems* 11:295–317.

———. 1984. Employee Assistance Programs. In *Research in Community Mental Health*. Vol. 4, edited by J. R. Greenberg. Greenwich, Conn.: JAI Press.

Trice, Harrison M., and George Ritzer. 1969. Role of Unions in Industrial Alcoholism Programs. *Addictions* 16:13–30.

Trice, Harrison M., and Paul M. Roman. 1978. *Spirits and Demons at Work.* 2d ed. Ithaca, N.Y.: ILR Press.

Trice, Harrison M., and Mona Schonbrunn. 1981. A History of Job-Based Alcoholism Programs: 1900–1955. *Journal of Drug Issues* 11:171–98.

Tyrrell, Ian R. 1979. *Sobering Up: From Temperance to Prohibition in Antebellum America, 1800–1860.* Westport, Conn.: Greenwood Press.

Van Maanen, John. 1986. Power in the Bottle: Drinking Patterns and Social Relations in a British Police Agency. In *Executive Power,* edited by Suresh Srivastiva. San Francisco: Jossey-Bass.

Van Maanen, John, and Stephen R. Barley. 1984. Occupational Communities: Culture and Control in Organizations. *Research in Organizational Behavior.* Vol. 6: 287–365.

Volpe, Joan. 1982. Flight Attendants' Subculture: An Ethnography. Unpublished research study. Washington, D.C.: Association of Flight Attendants.

Weisner, Constance, and Robin Room. 1984. Financing and Ideology in Alcohol Treatment. *Social Problems* 32(2):167–84.

Wilentz, Sean. 1984. *Chants Democratic: New York City and the Rise of American Working Class, 1788–1850.* New York: Oxford University Press.

Yin, Robert. 1984. *Case Study Research: Design and Methods.* Beverly Hills, Calif.: Sage.

Zenger, Todd, and Barbara Lawrence. 1989. Organizational Demography: The Differential Effects of Aging and Tenure Distributions on Technical Communication. *Academy of Management Journal* 32(2):353–76.